A GUIDE
WILD FOOD
FORAGING

Published 2023—IMM Lifestyle Books, an imprint of
Fox Chapel Publishing
903 Square Street,
Mount Joy, PA 17552
www.FoxChapelPublishing.com

Portions of *A Guide to Wild Food Foraging* (2023) are taken from *Self-Sufficiency: Foraging for Wild Foods* (2016), published by IMM Lifestyle Books, an imprint of Fox Chapel Publishing Company, Inc.

ISBN 978-1-5048-0135-5

Library of Congress Control Number: 2023934247

We are always looking for talented authors. To submit an idea, please send a brief inquiry to acquisitions@foxchapelpublishing.com.

Printed in China
10 9 8 7 6 5 4 3 2 1

A GUIDE TO
WILD FOOD
FORAGING

Proper Techniques for Finding and Preparing Nature's Flavorful Edibles

David Squire

IMM **lifestyle** ∴ books™
Read. Learn. Do What You Love.

Contents

Introduction

Today, most Western countries get their food from tenuous supply chains steeped in strict financial directives rather than from local farms and market gardens. This reliance on larger social and economic systems has led to both rising costs and empty shelves. Rather than accept this trend, many people have realized that self-reliant options are both cheaper and healthier. By becoming a forager—as well as perhaps starting to grow some of your own fruits and vegetables—you will be countering this trend and getting back to the basics of life.

Humans have a long history of foraging. It is impossible to know exactly when, but it certainly began in Africa among our bipedal ancestors, long before the successful exodus of our species into other parts of the world some 80,000 years ago. Later, hunter-gatherers in groups of 10 to 50 were adept at living off the land, surviving on animals they hunted, as well as eating leaves, berries, roots, fruits, and nuts. They wandered the land in search of seasonal food, sometimes following migratory herds, while coastal peoples used the resources offered by the sea.

Foraging can either be the first step in your journey or something you do for fun. But once you realize how simple and satisfying finding and cooking your own food can be, it's easy to find other ways to make your own resources, whether that's baking bread, sewing clothes, or raising animals. Foraging can be a great hobby or way of life because you get to soak up the outdoors, learn more about nature, and get nutritious foods at the end. It's time to take your first step!

Types of Foraged Foods

This forager's handbook is organized to enable readers to gain instant information. The following pages provide an extensive directory of plants (and some shellfish) that can be foraged. Over 100 species, both wild and escapees from gardens, are included, along with tips on identification, where to find them, what and when to harvest, and how to prepare and use what you find. It is divided into seven parts:

- **Edible wild plants**, include Chickweed, Dandelions, and Stinging Nettles, which are often the bane of gardeners. However, these are typically the ancestors of most vegetables used in the kitchen today. Others can easily swap out the greens used in salads and other dishes for a more robust flavor.

- **Popular wayside kitchen herbs** are often escapees from earlier herb gardens. These include Caraway, Fennel, and Spearmint. Foraging for these wild varieties provide you with fresh ingredients for your spice rack.
- **Wild fruits** can still be found in the wild, although many are widely grown as cultivated fruits. These include Blackcurrants, Cranberries, and Gooseberries. Unlike in supermarkets, these fruits are time-dependent, smaller, and typically easier to bruise. But they are a much sweeter reward!
- **Wild nuts**, borne by trees such as Beech, Hazel, and Oak, are edible and collectable. Being able to identify the tree is as important as knowing the fruit in this case. You might also see them growing in hedgerows.
- **Mushrooms, truffles, and other edible fungi** can be gathered and eaten. Most grow at soil-level, some on trees, and a few underground. For safety's sake, careful identification of all fungi is absolutely necessary.
- **Seaweeds** are gathered along shorelines, or just beneath low water, and provide highly nutritious meals. Though less common today, this was once a typical resource for our ancestors, and they are surprisingly versatile.
- **Shellfish**, including Clams, Cockles, and Winkles, can be collected from the wild. While they are the outlier in this group, shellfish are a delight to discover along the coast and incorporate into meals.

Foraging Code

These simple guidelines will make a big difference to plant life in your area.

- **Do not strip plants of all their leaves, fruits, or nuts.** Gather a few leaves, fruits, or nuts from each plant. Use a knife or scissors to remove them cleanly. Harvest fungi by carefully twisting the stem and then pulling slightly.
- **Do not remove flowers from annual or biennial plants** as the plant relies on these parts to produce new plants and fruits for the following year.
- **Do not dig up plants**—it's illegal.
- When searching for a plant, **do not trample over surrounding plants** as you may destroy them.
- Be aware that **many species of plants are endangered and rare**. Gather only those that you know grow in abundance, and do not over-forage. Leave most plants where you find them to benefit wild animals and insects.

The Use of Common and Botanical Names

Plants are arranged in alphabetical order according to their most popular common name within each chapter with the botanical name following. Additionally, because plants (and shellfish) are often native to wide areas of the world, they may have gathered many more common names, which are also listed. Therefore, if you only know the common name of a particular plant or shellfish, you will be able to find it in the index and then establish where it is described and illustrated. Additionally, where earlier botanical names are still used, these will be included as well—a great help where plants are known and identified through earlier floras and gardening books.

Most native plants have a multitude of common names but, surprisingly, coastal plants like Sea Purslane have fewer variations than plants that populate inland habitats. It is significant that plants notorious for their invasive habits, such as Ground Elder, have an abundance of common names throughout their habitats. Check your local offices for natural resources (including websites) to see if there are invasive species that they encourage foragers to pick. This way, you can eat delicious food while helping wildlife thrive!

Plant Conservation

The need to conserve and protect native plants for future generations is a responsibility we must all take seriously. Each year, hundreds of species of wild plants around the world are lost to us through habitat loss, greed on the part of some plant collectors, and ignorance. Whatever the cause, this trend needs to be halted. This book will help you identify plants and teach the proper method to forage them, but please do your research before you start foraging. Laws, ecosystems, and communities vary around the world, meaning it's best to know as much as possible so you don't contribute to the problem.

There are a number of places to forage for plants that may not initially occur to you. Apart from local fields, roadsides, and hedges, many other manmade places provide homes to plants. Towpaths along canals dug centuries ago are full of plants, while disused railways provide not only footpaths and cycle trails but also have become ribbons of flourishing plant life. Banking alongside highways also gives protection to plants, but plants along busy roads cannot be foraged for obvious reasons—the dangers of pollution and fast-moving traffic.

Correct Identification

It is essential to know precisely what you are gathering to avoid poisonous plants, and this applies equally to leafy plants as well as to fungi. Therefore, always be certain about the plants you gather and, if in doubt, leave them alone.

Correctly identifying and gathering plants are skills that take time to acquire. Where to look, the time of year the plants are available, and what parts to gather and eat safely are the main questions asked by foragers. But there are also issues of legality that need to be addressed when collecting plants from the wild (see page 10).

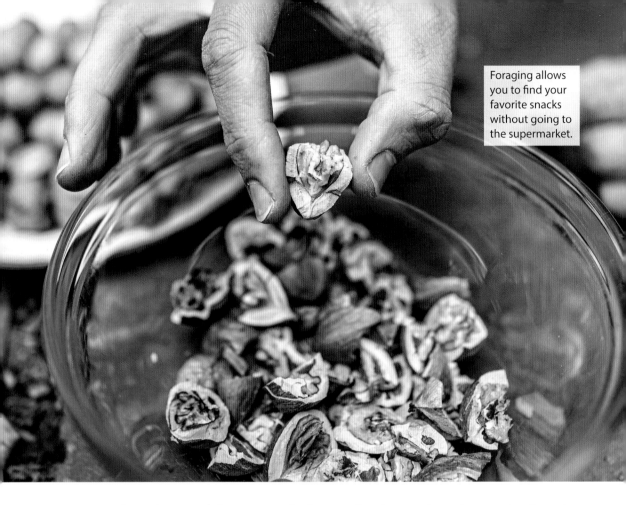

Foraging allows you to find your favorite snacks without going to the supermarket.

Try to begin foraging with someone who knows what they are doing; learning by observing on the spot with a knowledgeable guide is the best way to acquire safe foraging skills.

Questions of Legality

In many countries, wild plants are protected by the law and uprooting native plants is illegal, unless permission is first gained from the landowner or occupier. Additionally, permission is especially required to forage for wild plants in nature reserves, in national parks, on land owned by national land organizations, and on land owned by military establishments.

Wayside plants have long escaped the legality question and foragers are usually free to remove (in moderate amounts) flowers, leaves, fruits (berries and nuts), and fungi from verges and banks alongside town and country roads. Path edges can also be legally foraged.

Remember that foraging just a few plants for your own personal use is usually not a problem, but creating an industry from your gathering is questionable, and you would certainly need permission from the landowner or occupier.

Occasionally, you will come across signs that says, "Trespassers will be prosecuted." The intentions and liabilities of such signs vary from one country to another, and it has been suggested that they are meaningless in law unless actual damage is committed. However, to avoid problems arising needlessly, gain permission before foraging on private land. Always ask yourself if the land belonged to you, would you want people walking over it without permission?

After Gathering

Apart from identifying and gathering plants safely, getting them home intact requires care. Leaves need a wide basket that does not constrict them. Berries and nuts, however, need containers that can be closed to prevent them spilling and rolling out.

Cover your basket to prevent the sun and wind from drying your gatherings. Wash and dry leaves (if dirty) as soon as you get them home. Place them in a cool shaded room, away from direct and strong sunlight. Some plants and fruits do not require washing, and this is explained in the text for each plant.

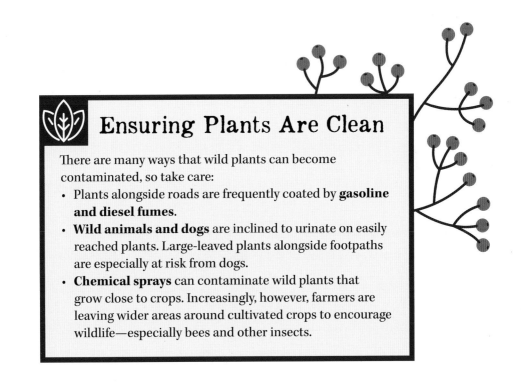

Ensuring Plants Are Clean

There are many ways that wild plants can become contaminated, so take care:

- Plants alongside roads are frequently coated by **gasoline and diesel fumes**.
- **Wild animals and dogs** are inclined to urinate on easily reached plants. Large-leaved plants alongside footpaths are especially at risk from dogs.
- **Chemical sprays** can contaminate wild plants that grow close to crops. Increasingly, however, farmers are leaving wider areas around cultivated crops to encourage wildlife—especially bees and other insects.

Edible Wild Plants

The major wild plants for foraging are represented here. Some are becoming rare in the wild even though they've been widely and intensively cultivated for centuries. When foraging, treat these rarer species—and all plants for that matter—with respect and restraint.

Among the wild plants fit for foraging are the ancestors of many of our modern-day vegetables. One of these is Wild Cabbage (see page 40); over several centuries and with careful selection by seed companies, it has yielded brassicas as diverse as Brussels Sprouts and Cauliflowers, as well as Cabbages, Kohlrabi, and Broccoli. Similarly, Spinach (see page 41) has left a legacy of vegetables, some with large and nutrition-packed swollen roots for feeding cattle, others useful for processing into sugar, as well as succulent and richly colorful roots for adding to salads.

In earlier centuries, because of their value as food crops, many native European plants were introduced to other countries by settlers. Most plants survived and flourished in these new habitats and, in some cases, were too successful. In New Zealand, for instance, introduced Watercress has become a serious problem when it blocks waterways.

Asparagus
(*Asparagus officinalis*)

Also known as: Common Asparagus, Wild Asparagus

A delicious and distinctive perennial with spreading roots that allow it to produce new stems each year. There are two forms and only the upright one, growing up to about 5' (1.5m), is abundant enough to be gathered. Its stiff stems are generously clad in needle-like cladodes—botanically speaking, flattened leaf-like stems—and from a distance have a fern-like appearance. Male flowers (yellow, tinged red at base) and female (yellow to white-green) are usually borne on separate plants from early to late summer. Round, red berries about ¼" (6mm) wide appear slightly later.

The upright form (*A. o.* ssp. *officinalis*) is native to the warmer parts of Europe, Asia, and North Africa, and is naturalized in all of the United States. It has been introduced into many other countries for cultivation as a food plant, from where it has escaped.

You'll find it: In grassy areas, especially in coastal regions, on cliffs or in dunes, and where the soil is light and well drained.

Spears: Edible parts of asparagus are the spear-like young shoots that appear in spring and through early or mid-summer. Asparagus in the wild is not so large and prolific as that grown in vegetable gardens that can be cut when about 9" (23cm) high.

Harvesting the spears: Only harvest in areas where there is a plentiful supply of spears (it is scarce in some areas). Where there are sufficient spears to harvest, use a long-bladed knife to cut the base just below soil-level.

Using the spears: Wash and recut the bases, then either steam or poach in water until just tender. Asparagus spears are versatile in the kitchen and can be used in many dishes, including fondues, risottos, quiches, soups, and salads. Asparagus is also delicious steamed and served simply, either drizzled with melted butter, a vinaigrette, or a hollandaise sauce.

Chickweed
(*Stellaria media*)

Also known as: Chicken's Meat, Chickenweed, Stitchwort

Birds and chickens love to peck at the flowers and seeds of this widespread and abundant sprawling annual, which persists throughout winter in mild climates. It spreads and forms masses of leaves on weak stems that creep over the soil, forming clumps up to 14" (35cm) but usually less.

The plant produces white, star-like flowers about ⅜" (9mm) across throughout the year, but mainly in summer. It is widely spread throughout the world and found in most countries, but is most abundant in Asia, Europe, north Africa, and throughout North America.

You'll find it: On bare ground, especially in light, cultivated soil where seeds quickly germinate and create carpets of leaves, stems, and flowers.

Leaves: The abundant soft, bright green, oval leaves clasp stems; as they age, they become darker and tougher.

Harvesting the leaves: If tugged sharply, whole stems complete with soil-covered roots are pulled up, so use sharp scissors to cut off only the young, leaf-clad stems. If they appear dirty, wash and allow to dry.

Using the leaves: Young leaves have a mild flavor and can be eaten raw in salads, when they are at their best. Young stems are just as tender as the leaves and can also be eaten, although some people remove them. Add the leaves to scrambled eggs, use in soups, or gently soften in butter, which makes their flavor resemble spring spinach.

In times of scarcity, Chickweed seeds have been ground to a fine powder and used to make bread or to thicken soups; the leaves were picked, dried, and infused in boiling water to make a tea.

Chicory
(*Cichorium intybus*)

Also known as: Barbe-de-Capuchin, Blue Daisy, Blue Endive, Blue-sailors, Bunk, Coffee Weed, Common Chicory, Succory, Wild Succory, Witloof

A well-known perennial with a long taproot and stiffly erect, grooved stems to 36" (90cm), chicory is native to many regions—much of Europe, western Asia, and North Africa. It now thrives in eastern Asia, North and South America, South Africa, Australia, and New Zealand. The roots are eaten as a vegetable, the leaves used in salads, and flowers as a garnish. The roots are also used as a coffee substitute.

You'll find it: In grassy areas and on waste ground, especially on chalk, alongside old vegetable gardens, community gardens, and near derelict country cottages.

Roots, leaves, and flower heads: The light-brown roots are 18" (45cm) or more long when in light, deeply cultivated soil, and somewhat shorter when growing in heavy soil. Basal leaves above the root's top are spear-shaped and stemless while upper ones clasp upright, stiff stems. Stems bear azure-blue daisy-like flowers from early summer to early autumn.

Harvesting the roots and leaves: Roots are best dug up in late autumn, when the leaves are dying down. However, unless you have permission from the landowner, it is illegal to dig up plants growing in the wild. Pick young, fresh leaves for salads, washing and drying before using. Flowers, for garnish, should be picked when young and fresh.

Using the roots and leaves: Apart from a coffee substitute, roots can be grated and added to salads, or eaten as a cooked vegetable; reduce their bitterness by boiling for the second time in fresh water. Some people, however, prefer the bitter taste.

Using the leaves: Add to summer salads.

Chicory Coffee

To use as a coffee substitute, clean, peel, and chop up the roots into 3" (7.5cm) long pieces, then roast under a grill until deep brown, firm, and crisp. When completely cool, grind the crisp roots in a coffee grinder or food processor to form coffee-like granules or powder.

Chicory is highly prized in some countries as it produces a coffee with a deep color and does not contain caffeine. Occasionally, it is blended with "true" coffee.

Comfrey
(*Symphytum officinale*)

Also known as: Back-wort, Boneset, Bruisewort, Church Bells, Common Comfrey, Healing Herb, Knitbone, Pigweed

Growing 48" (1.2m) high, comfrey is a bushy herbaceous perennial famed for its ability to grow in low temperatures and its prodigious yield of leaves, which are used to feed cattle. Its cream-white, mauve, yellow-white, or pink bell-shaped flowers are borne in clusters during late spring and early summer. Native to much of Europe and Asia, it has been taken to other countries as animal fodder and has escaped into the wild and become naturalized. It now thrives in North and South America and New Zealand. In addition to its fodder qualities, comfrey is widely recommended in country cures, including reducing pain, healing broken bones, as a poultice, and to relieve coughs.

You'll find it: Especially in damp areas alongside wet ditches, streams, and rivers; also, at the edges of fields where it was once cultivated.

Leaves: Masses of broad, spear-shaped, hairy-surfaced, mid-green leaves up to 10" (25cm) long.

Harvesting the leaves: Cut young leaves from plants and wash before use.

Using the leaves: When dipped in batter and fried, comfrey is claimed to be one of the tastiest delights for foragers. The stems and leaves can be boiled in the same way as cabbage. The older leaves have as much flavor as younger ones in cooked dishes, but the young leaves are picked in spring to add to salads.

Comfrey Soup

INGREDIENTS

- 1¾ tablespoons (25g) margarine or butter
- 3 tablespoons (25g) plain flour
- 2½ cups (600ml) milk
- 3–4 tablespoons comfrey leaves, finely chopped
- Stock cube (chicken or vegetable)
- 1¼ cups (300ml) water

INSTRUCTIONS

1. Make a white sauce as a base using margarine or butter, plain flour, and milk.
2. Add comfrey leaves, which have first been lightly cooked in butter as you would spinach.
3. Add a crumbled stock cube and water to the soup, then add seasonings to taste.
4. Bring the soup to a gentle boil and stir for a few minutes before serving with crusty bread or croutons.

Curled Dock
(*Rumex crispus*)

Also known as: Curly Dock, Narrow-leaf Dock, Sour Dock, Yellow Dock

An upright herbaceous perennial that grows to about 42" (1m) with stems of densely clustered tiny flowers from early summer to mid-autumn that turn a rich brown after they start to produce seeds. The shiny brown seeds have a covering that allows them to float on water as well as to be caught in wool and animal fur, enabling plants to spread easily and rapidly. Indeed, in some areas, this plant is treated as a pest as it invades cultivated crops.

It is seen all over Africa, Europe, and Asia, but has been naturalized in the United States and some parts of Canada.

You'll find it: In a wide range of habitats, including shingle beaches, sand dunes, on waste ground, cultivated soil, and in grassy areas.

Leaves: Dark green, lance-shaped, and wavy edged. Unlike some docks, the lower leaves are not distinctively heart-shaped at their bases.

Harvesting the leaves: Preferably cut at the base when the leaves are young, and use immediately before they wilt and become limp.

Using the leaves: Add fresh young leaves to salads—wash and dry first to ensure they are not contaminated by animals. Old leaves are usually too bitter to be eaten fresh but can be boiled in several changes of water to make them palatable; use these as a green vegetable.

Young leaves are often cooked like spinach to accompany ham or bacon; either blanch the leaves quickly in a little water or sauté with a tablespoon of butter, add a tiny amount of vinegar, and season with salt and pepper.

Edible Docks

Several related species are ideal for foraging, including Sorrel (see page 37). Other docks include *Rumex obtusifolius*, the **Broad-Leaved Dock**, with leaves that can be eaten when young but are usually more bitter than curled dock. It is also known as Butter Dock because its long, broad leaves were used to wrap around butter to keep it cool and fresh.

Monk's Rhubarb (*Rumex alpinus*, earlier known as *Rumex pseudoalpinus*) is native to central and southern Europe and parts of Asia. In the Middle Ages, it was used as a potherb, when young leaves were eaten fresh. It is now naturalized in many countries, including North America.

Dandelion
(*Taraxacum officinale*)

Also known as: Clock Flower, Clocks and Watches, Common Dandelion

This well-known perennial can be foraged for its leaves and for the roots that make a passable substitute coffee. Flowers are golden yellow, often 2" (5cm) or more across and borne singly at the tops of hollow, soft stems. Dandelion is found abundantly in North and South America, Europe, South Africa, Australia, and New Zealand, where it has been taken as a food plant and become naturalized.

You'll find it: In meadows, pastures, lawns, waste ground, gardens, and alongside roads.

Leaves and roots: Light green leaves, 10" (25cm) long that develop from the plant's base and reveal deeply indented edges.

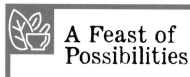

A Feast of Possibilities

Dandelions offer foragers even more prizes. In early summer, young roots can be boiled and added to salads, while young flower buds can be eaten fresh in salads or boiled. Mature flowers can be cooked in batter or used to brew dandelion wine (there are numerous recipes to be found in old cookery books and on the web).

Harvesting the leaves and roots: Snap off or cut young leaves from near the base; toward the end of summer, they toughen and are less appetizing. Harvest roots in autumn when fat and starting to harden. They are so common that you may well be able to dig them from your own garden. Avoid those along country paths and roadsides, since they may be contaminated by dogs and exhaust fumes.

Using the leaves and roots: Add young leaves to salads; wash thoroughly then trim off stem bases. By picking from young plants, it is possible to have salad leaves all summer.

Crispy bacon pieces added to a dandelion salad makes a delicious combination. To make coffee, gather roots, wash, and trim tops and bottoms. Do not peel, just brush under a tap until clean. Place in full sun to dry, then roast in a moderate oven until brittle. Grind coarsely. Many believe it is almost indistinguishable from real coffee, with the bonus of not containing caffeine.

Fat Hen
(*Chenopodium album*)

Also known as: Bacon Weed, Frost-blite, Goosefoot, Lamb's Quarters, Meal-weed, Pigweed, Wild Spinach, White Goosefoot

This common annual grows up to 24" (60cm) high, from widely scattered seeds produced by flowers that appear from early summer to mid-autumn. This unprepossessing plant has filled stomachs since early man roamed the landscape. It is widely naturalized in Africa, Australia, North America, and Oceania, and now grows almost everywhere in soils rich in nitrogen, especially on wasteland. It spreads readily and creates colonies.

You'll find it: On waste ground as well as in cultivated soil, along the edges of fields, on trash heaps, and the sides of ditches. It is abundant on disturbed soil, especially that which is friable and moisture-retentive, where the seeds germinate easily, and young plants grow.

Leaves and seeds: Pale gray-green leaves are usually lance-shaped but can be variable and with a diamond outline. Young leaves have a mealy-white covering, and rise directly from main stems that are usually green but sometimes reddish. The leaves are rich in iron, vitamins, and calcium. The small, black, round or kidney-shaped seeds are tightly clustered in spikes toward the top of stems. Individual plants can produce as many as 75,000 seeds.

Harvesting and using leaves and seeds: Gather young leaves and shoots in spring and early summer for cooking like spinach; use as a green vegetable or add to soups. Alternatively, use fresh in salads. Later in summer, young leaves can be used in a similar way; with age, those lower down become bitter and unpalatable. When gathering seeds, cut off entire stems with their seeds attached and put the heads upside down in a paper bag. Seeds will eventually fall off and can be gathered and used, either as a cereal or ground into a black flour and made into bread, which is highly nutritious.

Good King Henry
(*Chenopodium bonus-henricus*)

Also known as: All Good, Goosefoot, Lancashire Asparagus, Mercury, Perennial Goosefoot, Wild Spinach

This erect herbaceous perennial grows to 20" (50cm) high, with a bushy and slightly spreading nature, and is popular as a green vegetable. From late spring to mid-summer plants develop tapering and pyramidal heads of small green flowers. It is native to much of central and southern Europe and grows in the gardens of many countries, including North America.

Cooking Flower Buds and Young Shoots

Wash the buds and young shoots thoroughly and simmer in a saucepan for five minutes in just enough boiling water to cover. Alternatively, you could steam them to retain nutrients. Drain well, pour over some melted butter, and serve on toast.

You'll find it: Around old gardens, fields, and community gardens, along the sides of country roads, and especially in areas close to old cottages where it might earlier have been cultivated. It likes fertile, moisture-retentive soil.

Leaves: Normally up to 4" (10cm) long and clustered around upright stems, the leaves are somewhat fleshy, triangular, and a lustrous green.

Harvesting the leaves: Cut the leaves while young, throughout the summer, severing them at the base. Although it has a succulent nature, leaves soon go limp once picked; therefore, do not pick more leaves than you can use that same day.

Using the leaves: Trim off long stems from the bases of leaves and wash thoroughly under running water, then boil or steam in the same way you might cook spinach. Because of its high oxalic acid content, eat in moderation (although it is also rich in iron and vitamin C). Early in the year (usually during late spring and early summer), gather young shoots and steam or cook these in a similar way to asparagus.

Goosegrass
(*Galium aparine*)

Also known as: Bedstraw, Catchweed, Catch-weed Bedstraw, Cleavers, Clivers, Common Cleavers, Hairif, Hayriff, Sticky Willie

A sprawling annual with prostrate or scrambling branched stems up to 42" (1m) long, with groups of leaves at intervals along the stems. Small stems arise from the leaf joints and bear tiny, dull-white flowers from early to late summer. The stems have numerous small, downturned prickles that cling to clothing and fur, giving rise to many of the plant's common names.

It is found in the woods and thickets of most of North and South America, Europe, Asia, Australia, New Zealand, and scattered locations in Africa.

You'll find it: In hedges, on waste ground, in ditches, shady thickets, on cultivated land, and in coastal areas.

Leaves: At intervals along the stems, six to eight, light to mid-green, narrow and pointed leaves arise in clusters.

Harvesting the leaves: These are best when young and easily cut from the plant, together with their stems, with a sharp knife or scissors. If just pulled, the entire plant becomes dislodged. Cut and use the leaves and stems before the hard, round seeds appear.

Using the leaves: Boil both the leaves and stems in water for a few seconds to remove the plant's clinging nature and make the leaves and stems palatable. It can be used as a green vegetable and is very high in vitamin C—in earlier times, it was used to keep scurvy at bay. In the 17th century, the leaves and stems were recommended for use in desserts and spring soups.

♡ Coffee Substitute

The seeds of goosegrass can be roasted to produce a coffee substitute. Collect and dry the seeds well, then roast until brown in a medium oven. They can then be ground and used to make a hot drink.

Ground Elder
(*Aegopodium podagraria*)

Also known as: Ash-weed, Bishop's Gout-weed, Bishop's Weed, Farmer's Plague, Goat's Foot, Goutweed, Ground Ash, Herb Gerard, Parson's Weed, Snow-in-the-Mountain

To many people this is one of the most pernicious garden weeds. It has an herbaceous perennial nature, with creeping roots that enable it to spread and colonize land, therefore eating it can be considered an act of common justice! Growing to 42" (1m) or less, it has hollow stems that bear the leaves, and from early to late summer, white flowers in umbrella-like heads.

Found in the temperate zone of the Middle East and the whole mainland of Europe, it was originally introduced as a food and medicinal plant (invariably against gout). It is established throughout North America and many other countries, where initially it was cultivated as a potherb.

You'll find it: On waste grounds, especially near old buildings and gardens. Also look at the base of hedges and alongside roads.

Leaves: Are 4"–8" (10–20cm) long, medium to dark green, and usually formed of three finely tooth-edged leaflets.

Harvesting the leaves: Young leaves are the best and tastiest, picked in spring and early summer. However, pinching out flower shoots helps to protract the season when young leaves appear. Collect leaves before the plants flower, as after that time they have a strongly laxative nature.

Using the leaves: Wash the leaves thoroughly under running water, then allow to dry in the air. Ground elder leaves can be used in a wide range of dishes and preparations, including soups, quiches, fritters, and omelets. These can also be steamed and used much like spinach. Add young leaves to salads, where they impart an aromatic and rather tangy flavor.

Jack-by-the-Hedge
(*Alliaria petiolata*)

Also known as: Garlic Mustard, Garlic Root, Hedge Garlic, Jack in the Bush, Jack-in-the-Hedge, Penny Hedge, Poor Man's Mustard, Sauce Alone

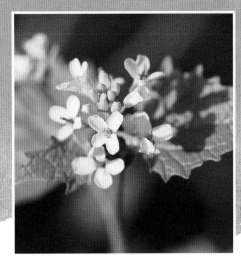

An erect annual or biennial with a slender taproot that smells strongly of garlic when crushed. In mild and warm areas, jack-by-the-hedge flowers in early spring, producing early seeds that fall and germinate later in the same year; these create a further display of plants, but this is not the norm. Clusters of white flowers appear at the tops of stems from mid-spring to early summer.

Native throughout Europe, southern Turkey, North Africa, and as far as the Caucasus and Himalayas, it has been introduced to many other areas, including the understory of North America from Canada to Virginia.

You'll find it: At the sides of hedges and walls, along the edges of woods, and in shaded gardens.

Leaves: Long-stemmed, bright green leaves with heart-shaped bases that emit a garlic-like aroma when bruised.

Harvesting the leaves: Cut off young leaves when wanted and use as soon as possible as these tend to wilt quickly. Each plant has only a few leaves so select only a very few at a time from each plant.

Using the leaves: Clusters of flowers, but primarily the leaves can be eaten fresh in spring and early summer salads. Additionally, the leaves can be used in a sauce to accompany lamb and herring. Create the sauce by chopping fresh young leaves together with a little mint, and mix with sugar and vinegar. The leaves can also be chopped and added to soups and meat casseroles.

Lovage
(*Levisticum officinale*)

Also known as: Cornish Lovage, Italian Lovage, King's Cumin, Old English Lovage

A tall herbaceous perennial about 4'–5' (1.2–1.5m) high with large, dark green leaves, it displays green-yellow flowers in large, umbrella-like heads from early to late summer.

Native to Mediterranean regions, the Balkans, India, and southern Asia, it has been taken to many warm and temperate countries as a culinary herb. Now it grows wild throughout central Europe, Asia, and the eastern United States.

You'll find it: In damp soil, often around neglected herb gardens and community gardens.

Leaves, stems, and seeds: The segmented leaves are large and formed of glossy, broad, coarsely toothed lobes, especially toward their tops. The stems are stiff and upright, while the yellow-brown seeds are egg shaped.

Harvesting the Leaves, stems, and seeds: Snip off the leaves while still young, together with young stems. Stems, which are hollow, can be candied and are therefore cut off slightly later. To gather seeds, wait until the flowers fade and the seeds are yellow-brown. Then, cut off the stems so that the seed heads can be placed upside down in a paper bag and the stems hung up. When dry, seeds will fall into the bag.

Using the Leaves, stems, and seeds: When young, use the leaves in salads, stir-fries, soups, and potato dishes. They can also be added to stews. Lovage butter, a fusion of butter, finely chopped leaves, plus pepper and salt is ideal as a dressing for corn on the cob.

Leaf stems when young are eaten fresh or candied. The seeds are used, whole or crushed, in cakes, biscuits, or sweets. Additionally, they are added to meat and cheese dishes and salad dressings to add flavor. Grated roots are ideal for adding to salads or cooked as a vegetable. It has a similar flavor to celery.

Meadowsweet
(*Filipendula ulmaria*)

Also known as: Maids of the Meadow, Meadow-sweet, Meadows Queen, Meadwort, Queen of the Meadow

An herbaceous perennial up to 48" (1.2m) high with long-stemmed leaves, meadowsweet has large, dense, umbrella-like heads of creamy-white flowers that emit a sweet but sickly fragrance from early summer to early autumn.

Native throughout Europe, from Iceland to Arctic Russia, Asia, and southern Turkey to Mongolia, it is seen as an escapee that has naturalized in eastern parts of North America.

You'll find it: In wet, damp woods and meadows; also, in marshes and fens and alongside streams and ditches.

Leaves: Pleasantly aromatic, dark green leaves, each formed of two to five pairs of tooth-edged leaflets. Leaves have gray-white undersides.

Harvesting the leaves: Cut while young and fresh and before eaten by insects.

Using the leaves and flowers: Chop up young leaves and use to flavor soups. Dried leaves have been used to introduce aromatics to wines as well as mead. Flowers, when added to beer and wine, are claimed to make a stronger and more heady brew, and introduces sweetness when used in cold drinks and fruit salads during summer.

 # Medicinal Values

Young leaves and flowers are occasionally infused together to make a tea that is claimed to ease the common cold, soothe inflammatory problems, and calm stomach complaints. The plant contains the chemicals that are used to produce aspirin.

Perennial Stinging Nettle
(*Urtica dioica*)

Also known as: Devil's Leaf, Devil's Plaything, European Nettle, Slender Nettle, Stinging Nettle, Tall Nettle

A well-known herbaceous perennial, 48" (1.2m) or more high, with tough yellow branching and spreading roots, it develops green flowers with yellow stamens in catkin-like arrangements from early to late summer. It is abundant in the countryside of northern Europe and much of Asia. In North America, it is found widely in Canada, the United States, and northernmost Mexico. It grows abundantly in the Pacific Northwest where the rainfall is high.

You'll find it: In hedgerows, on grassy banks and waste ground, in woods, and especially close to trash heaps and old abandoned buildings, where it forms near-impenetrable colonies.

Leaves: Upright stems, seldom branching, are covered with stinging hairs and bear green, somewhat heart-shaped, tooth-edged leaves that also impart a sting when touched.

Harvesting the leaves: Wear gloves and cut off the top 6" (15cm) of young stems only to the end of early summer; after that the leaves become tough, have a bitter taste, and laxative properties.

Using the leaves: Always wash the leaves under running water before preparing them for boiling or, preferably, steaming for about four minutes. These leaves, which are high in vitamins A and C, iron, and protein, can be used as a green vegetable as well as made into a purée—this is particularly good served on toast with the addition of a poached egg. Nettle soup is a delicious summertime forager's treat, and nettles can be included in any recipe that you would use spinach.

Nettle Soup

INGREDIENTS

- ½ brown paper grocery bag of nettle tops
- 2 onions, chopped
- 2 celery sticks, chopped
- 1 garlic clove, crushed
- 2 tablespoons butter
- 4¼ cups (1 L) vegetable or chicken stock
- 3–4 tablespoons crème fraiche or cream

INSTRUCTIONS

1. Collect nettle tops and leaves, then wash carefully.
2. In a large saucepan, soften onions, celery, and garlic clove in butter.
3. Add vegetable or chicken stock and all the nettles you can cram into your pan. Bring to the boil and simmer for 10 minutes or so until the nettles are tender.
4. Purée the soup in a blender or food processor, return to the pan briefly, and add crème fraiche or cream.
5. Heat through, add seasonings to taste, and serve.

Rock Samphire
(*Crithmum maritimum*)

Also known as: Samphire, Crest Marine, Rock Semper, Sea Bean, Sea Samphire

Succulent branching perennial with a slightly woody base, the plant can be recognized by its warm, slightly sulfurous scent. It grows 6"–15" (15–38cm) high, with a sprawling nature, especially if in a position open to the wind. The leaves are gray-green, with tiny, yellow-green flowers borne in umbrella-like arrangements from early to late summer.

It is found on coastlines throughout much of Europe, parts of the Middle East, and north Africa along the Atlantic, Mediterranean, and Black Sea coasts. It is also found in North America and Australia growing in herb gardens.

You'll find it: Usually on sea cliffs, in rocky, well-drained coastal areas, and occasionally in gravely and sandy soil.

Leaves: Firm and formed of several cylindrical, fleshy, narrow, tapering segments, each up to 2" (5cm) long.

Harvesting the leaves: Cut the leaf stems carefully, taking care not to pull them and to tear the plant from its roots. This is best done in spring or early summer before the flowers appear.

Using the leaves: Both the aromatic young leaves and their stems can be eaten. First, however, remove and discard those that have turned slimy, together with any hard parts on the stems. Wash the leaves thoroughly under running water and boil in water for about ten minutes or until soft, then eat as you would asparagus, with butter.

In earlier years, young leaves were especially prized and often pickled; they were first salted, then boiled, and soft-covered with spiced vinegar. Another recipe suggests pickling them with shallots, cloves, mace, and black mustard seeds to add further flavor. In some coastal areas, leaves were cooked and eaten with bread.

Salad Burnet
(*Sanguisorba minor*)

Also known as: Burnet, Drum Sticks, Garden Burnet, Old Man's Pepper, Poor Man's Pepper

This upright herbaceous perennial grows 6"–24" (15–60cm) high and from late spring to late summer develops rounded flower heads about ½" (1cm) wide, packed with green-white flowers, often with purplish tinges. However, it is the leaves that are the main culinary attraction.

It is native to large parts of Europe, North Africa, the Canary Islands, and southwest and central Asia; it was introduced into North America by early European settlers and has become widely naturalized and found on humid hillsides, mountains, and woodlands of North and South America, Australia, and New Zealand.

You'll find it: In dry, grassy places, especially where the soil is chalky.

Leaves: Formed of four to twelve pairs of gray-green leaflets with coarsely saw-toothed edges. When crushed, they emit the refreshing aroma of cucumbers.

Harvesting the leaves: Young leaves have the best flavor, becoming bitter as they age. Use as fresh as possible, before the leaves start to wilt.

Using the leaves: If dirty, wash in clean water and allow to dry. Use whole in salads and added to cool summer drinks, especially in punches, where their cucumber-like flavor has a cooling influence.

The leaves of this distinctive plant have many other uses, including chopped and added to soups, in sauces for fish dishes, and in casseroles. Additionally, leaves are used in vinegars and salad dressings, as well as finely cut up and sprinkled over steamed vegetables. It combines well with Rosemary (see page 62) and Tarragon.

Scotch Lovage
(*Ligusticum scoticum*)

Also known as: Lovage, Scots Lovage, Sea Lovage, Sea Parsley

This herbaceous perennial, growing up to 36" (90cm) high, has ribbed stems, usually green but occasionally tinted magenta-purple at the base, and has a celery-like aroma when crushed. Umbrella-like heads, up to 2½" (6cm) across, bear green-white to yellow flowers during early and mid-summer. The egg-shaped seeds are ridged. It is native to northern Europe, as far north as the Arctic Circle, Greenland, and North America. It can be found near the coasts of northern Europe and northeastern North America.

You'll find it: On rocky cliffs and on shingle beaches close to the seashore.

Leaves: Up to 4" (10cm) long and formed of five to ten oval segments, sometimes lobed. Like the stems, the coarsely tooth-edged, bright green, shiny leaves have a strong celery-like scent.

Harvesting the leaves: Snip off only a few at a time because this plant is scarce in some areas.

Using the leaves and stems: In earlier years, this robust plant was grown as a potherb, and during times of scarcity, the leaves have sustained people and helped to avert scurvy. Shred young leaves, add to early summer salads, and use to add body to soups. The leaves can also be wrapped around joints of meat for roasting. In a similar way to Angelica, the hollow stems can be candied, blanched, and stewed.

In earlier years, the seeds were added to soups, stews, and meat to add a sharp, hot flavor. Indeed, using seeds as a flavoring was popular when pepper was expensive.

Sea Kale
(*Crambe maritima*)

Also known as: Scurvy Grass, Sea Cabbage, Sea Colewort, Seakale

This cabbage-like perennial has erect stems about 36" (90cm) high, and fleshy roots that send up young shoots that are much sought after by foragers. However, only take a few shoots as these plants are relatively scarce in the wild.

The large lower leaves, up to 12" (30cm) long, are fleshy and rounded with crinkly lobes and irregularly toothed edges. The upper leaves are smaller, usually narrow, and without indentations. Lax and open clusters of white flowers with green claws appear from early to late summer.

It can be found along the coasts of mainland Europe and the British Isles to the Baltic Sea, as well as the Black Sea coasts of Bulgaria, Romania, Turkey, and Ukraine.

You'll find it: On cliffs, along coastal sands, and at the tops of shingle beaches.

Leaf stems: These are the desired parts and often become naturally blanched when sand and shingle are swept around the bases. In earlier years, local people waited for the first signs of it in late winter and early spring and then drew sand and shingle around the bases to cause blanching. This both whitened the stems and decreased their bitterness. It can be cut and eaten in late spring and early summer.

Harvesting the leaf stems: Cut young, clustered leaf stems when about 5"–6" (13–15cm) high, using a sharp knife to sever the stem fractionally below the ground's surface. Preferably, these young shoots are cut when the leaves are barely developed.

Using the leaf stems: These have a nutty and slightly bitter flavor and are usually cut into 3" (7.5cm) lengths and boiled in salted water until tender (15–20 minutes) or steamed like asparagus for five or so minutes until al dente. Serve with a butter sauce or lemon juice. Very young shoots can be shredded and eaten fresh in salads.

Sea Purslane
(*Atriplex portulacoides*)

You might find this well-branched, small evergreen shrub with creeping roots listed as *Halimione portulacoides* or even *Obione portulacoides* in old floras and gardening books. It has a spreading nature with branches creeping and developing roots at their stem joints.

From mid-summer to early autumn, it develops terminal clusters of flowers in short, branching spires. When in bud, they are reddish but soon turning green. However, it is the golden-yellow pollen that gives the plant a bright appearance. It is native throughout the sea shores of Europe from Denmark southward, and found around the Mediterranean Sea, from Europe to the Middle East. It has been introduced into North America, where it has colonized large areas near the Atlantic coast.

You'll find it: In salt marshes, alongside coastal water channels, and at the edges of salty pools. It also survives when flooded with seawater at high tide.

Leaves: Oval, mealy-covered, fleshy and gray-green, with silvery undersides. These are borne on upright, brownish stems to about 30" (75cm), but usually slightly less.

Harvesting the leaves: Cut young, fleshy leaves individually, taking care not to damage the plant by taking too many leaves.

Using the leaves: Trim off hard basal parts and wash thoroughly in running water to remove any excess salt and tideline debris. They are small and have a crunchy texture. Either eat raw in salads or stir-fry to accompany meat and fish dishes; however, take care not to cook excessively as this destroys the texture. In the past, it was grown as a potherb so that the young leaves could be readily picked.

Sorrel
(*Rumex acetosa*)

Also known as: Bread and Cheese, Common Sorrel, Garden Sorrel, Green Sorrel, Sour Dock, Spinach Dock

This erect, herbaceous perennial grows to about 42" (1m) with a clump-forming nature and has masses of arrow-shaped leaves. From late spring to late summer, it develops slightly branched stems bearing spires of small red and green flowers. For centuries, it has been eaten as a green vegetable, largely because of its lemon-like flavor.

It is found in grassland habitats throughout Europe, from the northern Mediterranean coast to the north of Scandinavia, as well as parts of Central Asia, New Zealand, Australia, and North America.

You'll find it: In grasslands, meadows, and open woodland; also along roadsides and in ditches.

Sorrel Sauce

Creating recipes for sorrel sauces appears to have been a cottage industry in earlier years. Many were created to serve with fish, utilizing the cooling, lemony flavor of the leaves to produce a green sauce. Leaves were chopped and boiled with very little water, then mixed with sugar and vinegar. A sauce made solely from the leaves was used to accompany pork or goose when apples were scarce.

Leaves: Up to 4" (10cm) long with an arrow-like outline; each leaf has distinctive downward-pointing lobes as its base. High in vitamin C and oxalic acid (which can be toxic in high doses).

Harvesting the leaves: Cut the stems of young leaves at the base; this gives later emerging leaves a better chance to develop. Use the leaves as soon as possible before they wilt.

Using the leaves: Apart from being used as a green vegetable, it can be cut and added fresh to salads, where it introduces a lemony flavor. Additionally, it is delicious in soups and sauces. Its versatility does not end there, as earlier it was a substitute for apple in tarts and turnovers. Puréed sorrel has been a popular accompaniment to veal and fish, as well as being added to omelets and stews.

Watercress
(*Rorippa nasturtium-aquaticum*)

Also known as: Bilders, Butter Cress, Tang-tongues, Tongue Grass

This popular and widespread perennial (occasionally annual), which is also called *Rorippa officinale* and *Nasturtium officinale*, has leaves and stems that are eaten fresh or occasionally boiled. Growing in water, the smooth, angular stems are anchored and secured by roots, while the hollow stems enable the upper parts to float. From late spring to mid-autumn, plants produce white-petaled flowers in upward clusters.

Native to southern and central Europe, including much of southern Scandinavia and the Carpathians, North Africa, and western Asia, it was introduced into many other countries including North and South America and New Zealand, and is most notably found in the United Kingdom.

You'll find it: In shallow streams and ditches with moving water or on their banks.

Leaves: Silky-green and broadly elliptical or round, with uncut edges; the lower leaves have one to three leaflets, while upper ones reveal five to nine, sometimes more. There are several closely related species, but this one has leaves that remain green in autumn, although it is susceptible to damage from winter frost.

Harvesting the leaves: Snip off young stems and leaves (do not pull as you may disturb the roots). Be aware that in some areas wild watercress may harbor liver flukes, a harmful parasite.

Using the leaves: Wash under a running tap. Do not pick leaves from plants in dirty ditches or those into which farm waste may have drained. Use the leaves while fresh, either as a nibble, in salads and sandwiches, or as a garnish. Leaves are especially high in vitamin C and iron. In earlier years, it was lightly boiled and used as a green vegetable. It has also been added to stews and soups (where it imparts a pungent flavor), chopped, and added to scrambled eggs, or stir-fried with other vegetables.

White Mustard
(*Sinapis alba*)

Also known as: Mustard

Known earlier as *Brassica alba* and *Brassica hirta*, this annual is often raised to produce young seedlings to accompany Garden Cress in the popular duo "mustard and cress"; they are used in sandwiches and salads and as a garnish. But the forager often finds that the plant is more developed, with larger distinctive leaves rather than seedlings.

In the wild, stems grow to about 30" (75cm) long, sometimes branched and sprawling. From early to late summer, plants develop lax and spire-like heads of lemon-yellow flowers.

Probably native to Mediterranean and western Asia, it is now widespread in Europe, Japan, North and South America, and New Zealand.

You'll find it: In moisture-retentive cultivated soil and waste ground; often an escapee from cultivation when grown as a food crop for animals or grown as a green manure crop that is later ploughed in to improve soil structure and nutritional qualities. Therefore, look for it at the edges of farmland and in ditches.

Leaves, flower buds, and seeds: Dull green leaves, stiff and hairy, deeply lobed, and up to 6" (15cm) long. As they age, the leaves become slightly bitter. The flower buds are borne on spikes and the seeds are produced in pods containing yellow-brown seeds.

Harvesting the leaves, flower buds, and seeds: Pick a few clean leaves for casual eating or a few more for taking home. Wash thoroughly and dry before use. Flower buds should be collected before the flowers open. Seeds are collected once the pods have developed and ripened.

Using the leaves, flower buds, and seeds: Lightly steam or stir-fry both leaves and flower buds, although leaves are best when fresh in salads. The seeds can be used to make mustard or to sprout for use in salads.

Wild Cabbage
(*Brassica oleracea*)

Also known as: Sea Cabbage, Sea Cole

This biennial or perennial is the ancestor of our cultivated European brassicas, ranging from Broccoli, Brussels Sprouts, and Cauliflowers to Kohlrabi. Although these food plants are certainly distinctive and markedly different from each other, when seen in flower, the similarities to their ancestor are readily apparent.

Wild cabbage usually grows no more than 42" (1m) high, with lax but clustered spires of yellow flowers from late spring to late summer. It grows mostly on the coasts of Europe, northern Africa, southern Asia, and the northwest coast of the United States. Sometimes plants similar to Wild Cabbage can be seen, but these are usually escapees from cultivated forms that have reverted to earlier characteristics.

You'll find it: As some of its common names suggest, it is a maritime plant and widely seen on cliffs, clinging to the sides and tops. It is also found around rocks and on dry-stone walls in coastal areas where it clings tenuously to life.

Leaves: Those at the base of the plant tend to have stems, are broad, rounded, and with lobes. They are slightly thick and fleshy, a characteristic that distinguishes them from related plants, such as White Mustard (see page 39) and other related species. The upper leaves partly clasp the stem and do not have lobes. Both types of leaves are gray-green.

Harvesting the leaves: Cut leaves off close to the base of the stem. Note that this plant is now scarce, so take only a very few leaves at one time.

Using the leaves: At one time, Sea Cabbage was so abundant that it was collected and sold from market stalls. Leaves can be steamed for use as a green vegetable, but they are more usually eaten fresh in spite of their bitter taste.

Wild Spinach
(*Beta vulgaris* ssp. *maritima*)

Also known as: Sea Beet

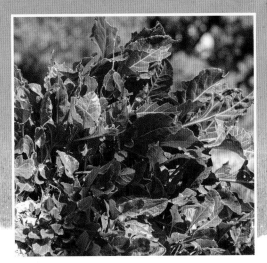

Known earlier as *Beta maritima*, this perennial is the ancestor of the many beets that are now grown for animal food, for sugar production, and for culinary purposes. Unlike culinary beetroots, Wild Spinach does not have conspicuously swollen areas at the junction of the roots and stems. Instead of being foraged for its roots, its large, fleshy leaves are much sought-after.

Plants grow 30"–36" (75–90cm) high and have narrow spires of tiny green flowers from mid-summer to early autumn. It can be found near the sea in Europe, northern Africa, and southern Asia. It grows on the coasts of the British Isles.

You'll find it: Either on the shore or close to shorelines.

Leaves: Thick and leathery oval or wedge-shaped and pointed shiny green, often 4" (10cm) or more long.

Harvesting the leaves: From late spring to early autumn, use a sharp knife to cut leaves cleanly, close to the base of each leafstalk. It is wise to select leaves that are on plants inaccessible to dogs.

Using the leaves: Wash leaves thoroughly. If old and have a pronounced central rib down the center, cut this away. Eat the leaves fresh, shredded, and added to salads, as well as cooked as a green vegetable in a similar way to spinach. Young leaves from near the plant's top are best for adding to salads. When cooking large leaves, steam rather than boil. Serve with two tablespoons of butter.

Wild Spinach and Lemon Salad

This is a popular recipe that reveals the tangy flavor of wild spinach.

INGREDIENTS

- Handful of wild spinach
- 1 cup (200ml) water
- Lemon
- Sprigs of watercress
- Olive oil, to taste
- Black pepper, coarsely ground, to taste

INSTRUCTIONS

1. Thoroughly wash the leaves and cut away tough stems and central parts.
2. Poach the leaves in boiling water for two to three minutes, then rinse in cold water.
3. After washing a lemon, slice it paper-thin and position slices around the edge of a plate.
4. Add the wild spinach and watercress.
5. Drizzle with olive oil and black pepper to finish the dish.

Popular Wayside Kitchen Herbs

Wayside kitchen herbs are a cosmopolitan group of plants native to large parts of the world, particularly the temperate zones that offer a warm and mild environment. Many of these herbs have been grown for thousands of years to add a wide spectrum of flavors to food and to provide herbal remedies.

These culinary delights differ widely in their growth habits and include annuals, biennials, and herbaceous perennials, as well as those with a shrub-like nature. Annual plants reproduce themselves from seeds produced every year, while biennials take two seasons to produce seeds. Herbaceous perennials last from one year to another—the leaves and shoots die down to soil-level in autumn or early winter, and in spring produce fresh growth. They owe their perennial nature to their hardy roots and stem bases.

Shrubs have a woody nature and can be evergreen or deciduous. Each shrub has several stems that arise from its roots to form a permanent framework. Rosemary is an excellent example of an evergreen, culinary shrub.

Because many of the culinary herbs featured here have been cultivated for centuries, it is not surprising that they have escaped and colonized areas around houses. Additionally, you might come across them in gardens and areas where old houses have been demolished and all that remains are skeleton walls and fences. Therefore, herbs can act as a record of an earlier cultivated past in what appears to be barren territory.

Borage
(*Borago officinalis*)

Also known as: Burrage, Cool-tankard, Talewort

This stout hollow-stemmed annual, growing to 18"–36" (45–90cm), bears clustered heads of sky blue, five-petalled, star-like flowers from early to late summer. There are also pink and white-flowered forms. Both the leaves and the flowers are covered in bristly hairs.

Native to North Africa and central Europe, it is found in gardens throughout Europe, especially France, Germany, Denmark, and the United Kingdom. It is also found in North and South America. Borage has a long history of medicinal and culinary use.

You'll find it: In well-drained soil with a sunny, warm aspect. It is more abundant in light soils than in heavy ones. Each year, it readily grows from self-sown seeds and often forms large colonies, especially around old herb gardens and community gardens.

Leaves: Oblong to oval dull-green leaves have a corrugated surface covered in rough white hairs. The lower leaves are 4"–6" (10–15cm) long, but those higher up the plant are half that size.

Harvesting the leaves: Pick when young and fresh before they harden, and use as soon as possible.

Using the leaves and flowers: Leaves have a flavor reminiscent of cucumber and can be infused to make a refreshing drink. Add both leaves and flowers to salads and fruit cups; the flowers can be candied. Before the introduction of cucumbers, the leaves of borage were used to flavor claret cups (borage is still added to that summer favorite, Pimm's). Leaves and stems were added to tankards of ale to introduce coolness and young leaves and shoots were used as a potherb during times of scarcity.

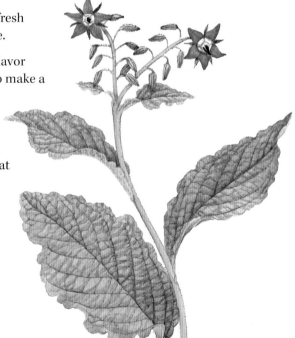

Caraway
(*Carum carvi*)

This hardy biennial, native to a wide area from Europe to Siberia, is primarily grown for its seeds. Caraway is a hollow-stemmed, much-branched plant with masses of feathery, fern-like, mid-green leaves that impart an aniseed-like flavor. It grows throughout the United States, from Canada to Greenland, and in northern Africa.

During early and mid-summer, small green flowers appear in umbrella-like heads at the tops of 24"–30" (60–75cm) high, upright stems on two-year-old plants.

You'll find it: At the edges of old and neglected herb gardens and community gardens. It is usually found in sunny positions and light well-drained but moisture-retentive soil.

Seeds: After the small white-pink flowers fade, seeds slowly appear. These are about ⅛" (3mm) long and mature to a gray-brown color.

Harvesting the seeds: As soon as seeds start to ripen, at the end of early summer and into mid-summer, cut off a few stems from a plant. Remember to leave a few flower heads on the plant to produce seeds that will later fall to the ground and create further plants. Tie several stems together and hang upside down in a large paper bag in a dry, cool, airy place until the seeds are dry and fall off the flower heads. When all seeds have fallen, pass through a sieve to remove fine, dust-like material that may have been attached to them.

Using the seeds: Used to flavor cakes, bread, and rolls, as well as for adding to salads and cheese dishes. They are also superb for introducing flavor to roast pork and lamb, as well as giving more flavor to sausages and cabbage. Store the seeds in dry, air-tight, clean jars; don't forget to add a label as seeds from different species often look similar. Young leaves are especially useful for introducing an aniseed flavor to soups.

Chamomile
(*Chamaemelum nobile*)

Also known as: Common Chamomile, Garden Chamomile, Russian Chamomile

Earlier known as *Anthemis nobilis*, this mat-forming, creeping perennial has been used instead of grass to create beautifully aromatic lawns. Nowadays, chamomile lawns are created from the variety 'Treneague,' which is non-flowering and needs little clipping to keep it low and tidy. The mid-green, finely dissected, somewhat moss-like aromatic leaves have a fruity scent when bruised and yield an essential oil.

Common Chamomile is native to southern and western Europe, North Africa, and the Azores. It has been taken to many warm and temperate countries, including North America, where it has escaped into the countryside. It grows in dry fields and around gardens across Europe and North and South America.

You'll find it: Along roadsides, sandy and well-drained commons, and pastures.

Petals: Plants 4"–12" (10–30cm) high display daisy-like flowers with white petals and yellow centers, singly on long stems from early to late summer.

Harvesting the petals: Collect flowers when fully open (usually during mid- and late summer) or when the petals are starting to turn down; use scissors to snip them off close to the stem's base.

Using the petals: An infusion of 1 oz. (25g) of flowers to a pint of boiling water makes a soothing tea. If you want to be able to make this drink out of season, pick the flowers and dry them on pieces of paper in a warm, well-ventilated room. When the heads are papery, place in dry, screw-topped jars; they keep well for several months.

Wild Chamomile

Known as *Matricaria recutita*, or earlier as *Matricaria chamomilla*, **Wild Chamomile** is an annual with light green, finely dissected leaves that emit an apple-like scent when bruised. White, daisy-like flowers appear in mid- and late summer and can be used in the same way as the perennial form of chamomile.

Chervil
(*Anthriscus cerefolium*)

Also known as: Salad Chervil

Biennial or annual in nature, this culinary herb is native to the Caucasus, the Middle East, and Russia, but now grows throughout most of the world, including northeast parts of North America. Growing 12"–18" (30–45cm), its ridged, hollow stems produce a strongly aniseed aroma when bruised. Note that the highly poisonous Hemlock and Fool's Parsley have similar characteristics to Chervil, so make certain you know what you are gathering.

When growing as a biennial, the plant produces umbrella-like heads, up to 3" (7.5cm) across, of white flowers from early to late summer in its second year.

You'll find it: Around old neglected and abandoned gardens and on hedge banks. It grows well in all soils, in full sunlight, or shade.

Leaves: Bright green and fern-like, resembling those of parsley. With age, they assume deeper shades of green and become tough.

Harvesting the leaves: Take only a few leaves at a time from each plant, so that it can continue to make healthy growth.

Using the leaves: Use in sandwiches and to garnish and flavor salads, soups, egg, and fish dishes. Chervil is a constituent of *fines herbes*, along with parsley, chives, and tarragon. Leaves can be dried slowly in slight warmth and used in stuffings.

Freezing Herbs

Along with other herbs—including parsley, basil, chives, and mint—young chervil leaves can be frozen. They retain their flavor, although once thawed, are limp and therefore best used for flavoring food, rather than as a garnish.

Always choose young, clean, and pest- and disease-free leaves for freezing. There are two ways to freeze these types of herbs:

- Pick young leaves, put loosely in freezer bags, and seal securely. Place these bags in rigid containers to prevent the leaves from being squashed, then place in a freezer.

- Chop up young, clean leaves, place in ice-cube trays, top up with water, and freeze. You can then add the frozen cubes directly to food during cooking.

With both freezing methods, all these herbs are best used within six months of freezing.

Chives
(*Allium schoenoprasum*)

Also known as: Ail Civitte, Cive, Ezo-negi, Schnittlauch

Hardy, clump-forming, tuft-based perennial with edible leaves. Additionally, during early and mid-summer, it has a decorative quality with bell-shaped lilac flowers crowded in a dense umbel and borne at the tops of upright stems 6"–8" (15–20cm) high. It is found abundantly in nature across temperate areas of Europe, Asia, and North America, and is widely cultivated as a culinary herb.

You'll find it: Because it is clump-forming, after some time in cultivation, plants are dug up and divided, with older parts from the center discarded and young pieces from around the outside replanted. For this reason, it is seen as an escapee around old heaps of soil or on old trash heaps where discarded clumps have been thrown. Look out for it at the edges of community gardens or old vegetable gardens.

Leaves: Grass-like, tubular, and mid-green with a delicate and mild onion-like flavor.

Harvesting the leaves: Rather than tearing from the plant's base, use scissors or a sharp knife to sever as low down as possible. Always choose the younger leaves and do not remove all the stems from one plant.

Herb of Legends

The Romans spread chives throughout much of their empire, believing that it could ease the pain of a sore throat and relieve sunburn. Later, it was claimed that a bunch of dried chives, when hung around a house, warded off evil spirits and diseases.

Using the leaves: Their mild onion flavor makes the leaves ideal in omelets, soups, egg, and cheese dishes; they also bring extra flavor to sandwiches. Use finely chopped chives as a garnish for mashed potatoes, and add to small boiled new potatoes, meat pies, and steak puddings.

The leaves can also be used in *fines herbes* and in tartare sauce. It is also a welcome addition to yogurt-based sauces and dips, such as tzatziki. Leaves can be frozen in the same way suggested for Chervil (see page 50). The flowers make a pretty garnish in salads.

Coriander
(*Coriandrum sativum*)

Also known as: Chinese Parsley, Cilantro

This distinctive culinary herb has erect stems and a branching nature together with fern-like dark-green leaves. Throughout summer, it displays pink-mauve or white flowers borne in umbrella-like heads. Its height varies from 9"–30" (23–75cm); therefore, it sometimes becomes lost among other escapees from cultivation. It is a hardy annual and each year increases itself from seeds.

An additional quality is its aromatic, ridged, initially green fruits that enclose seeds widely used as culinary flavorings. It originated in the Mediterranean and now grows widely across southern Europe and the Middle East. It also grows in many of the United States and in parts of South America in herb gardens and in wild places.

You'll find it: In bare patches around old herb gardens where it slowly colonizes large areas—but not densely. It prefers light soil and a warm and sheltered spot away from cold winds.

Leaves and seeds: Leaves have a bug-like scent when young and especially if bruised, but with age this disappears to reveal a sweet, spicy fragrance. Similarly, the seeds adopt a rich spiciness.

Harvesting the leaves and seeds: Cut the leaves when young and use before they wilt and dry. Sever the stems of flower heads when the fruits have turned from green to gray. Place upside down in paper bags so that the fruits will be caught and retained and dry slowly in gentle warmth. Rub to expel the seeds, which can be stored whole or ground to powder and stored in air-tight glass jars. Use within a year.

Aromatic Oil

The seeds are a source of an essential oil, which is used to flavor food, employed as a carminative, and in used in perfume and soap manufacturing. The oil is extracted by steam distillation.

Using the leaves and seeds: The spicy leaves can be added to broths, soups, meat dishes, and salads, while the seeds introduce a distinctive taste to curries and stews.

Dill
(*Anethum graveolens*)

Also known as: Dillweed

This hardy annual, earlier known as *Peucedanum graveolens*, is widely grown in herb gardens and is often seen as an escapee. Growing 24"–36" (60–90cm) high, it has an upright nature with hollow, ridged stems.

Native to sunny parts of Europe and southwest Asia, it is now naturalized in many warm regions, including the West Indies, southern parts of North America, Australia, and New Zealand. It reproduces itself by self-sown seedlings and, as an escapee, has colonized many other countries.

You'll find it: Around the edges of old and abandoned herb gardens, especially where the soil is light and the position warm and sunny.

Leaves and seeds: The blue-green, thread-like, feathery leaves that appear during summer have a distinctive aniseed flavor. From early to mid-summer, it bears small, yellow, star-like flowers in umbrella-like heads about 3" (7.5cm) wide. These flowers later produce small, brownish, slightly flattened seeds with thin, yellow ridges.

Harvesting the leaves and seeds: Cut off young leaves throughout summer, but take care not to defoliate plants. The leaves are difficult to dry but can be frozen in the same way as Chervil (see page 50). Gather the umbrella-like seed heads when the fruits change from green to brown, and place inside paper bags. They can be gathered and stored in air-tight containers, where they keep well for up to a year.

Using the leaves and seeds: Newly gathered leaves need to be used while still fresh as garnishes and flavoring for fish, boiled potatoes, beans, peas, poultry, and soups. They can also be added to salads. Seeds are added to vinegar when making pickles and add a sharpness to sauces.

Dippy Dill

INGREDIENTS
- 1 tablespoon dill, finely chopped
- 1 garlic clove, crushed
- Black pepper, to taste
- 1 cup (250ml) plain yogurt

INSTRUCTIONS
Add dill, garlic, and black pepper to plain yogurt to make a quick summer dip for *crudités*. Dill also goes remarkably well with poached or grilled salmon.

Fennel
(*Foeniculum vulgare*)

This hardy herbaceous perennial native to the shores of the Mediterranean but now widely naturalized across many of the world's dry soils near the coast and on riverbanks grows 7' (2m) or more high. It often appears as a haze of finely narrow leaves held on a framework of stiff, upright stems. It is sometimes confused with Dill (see page 54), but grows taller, has a perennial nature, and finer leaves. It is also somewhat similar to the highly poisonous Hemlock, so be certain of what you are gathering.

You'll find it: Old herb gardens and community gardens, as well as on waste ground, especially if the soil is slightly damp and moisture-retentive. It is also found in coastal areas and among old heaps of soil, where it has become naturalized.

Leaves and seeds: The thread-like, bright green to blue-green aromatic leaves appear in spring or early summer, with golden-yellow flowers packed in 4" (10cm) wide umbrella-like heads during mid- and late summer, and sometimes later in warm, mild summers.

Harvesting the leaves and seeds: Pick young leaves fresh throughout summer, taking care not to decimate plants. Leaves cannot be dried but can be frozen in the same way as Chervil (see page 50). Gather seed heads in late autumn just before they are fully ripe. Spread seeds on white paper and allow them to dry naturally in gentle warmth. Store in airtight jars for up to a year.

Using the leaves and seeds: Leaves are used to flavor egg and fish dishes, as well as in risottos, salads, and with vegetables. The strongly aniseed-flavored seeds are added to breads, cakes, soups, Italian sausages, and meatballs. The seeds are also widely used to make an effective digestive tea.

Confusing Namesake

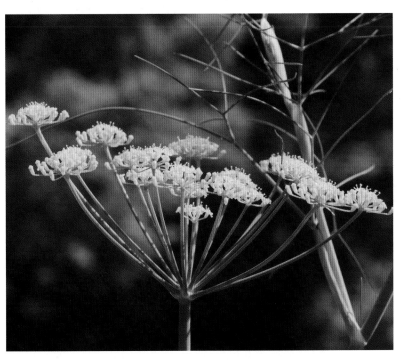

Apart from Fennel, there is **Florence Fennel**, sometimes known as Finocchio and botanically as *Foeniculum vulgare* var. *dulce*. It grows as an annual, has a similar but shorter appearance to Fennel, and a bulbous base to its stem. These stem-bases have a sweet, aniseed-like flavor, and are used raw in salads and cooked as a vegetable. Alternatively, they can be braised in stock to add further flavor.

Horseradish
(*Armoracia rusticana*)

Also known as: Great Railfort, Mountain Radish, Red Cole

Earlier known as *Cochlearia armoracia*, this popular hardy herbaceous perennial is famed for its pungently flavored roots. Its large, rough-surfaced, dark green, dock-like leaves have lobed or wavy edges and grow to about 18" (45cm) long. Small, white, cross-shaped flowers appear from late spring to late summer on long stems often hidden among the leaves. But it is the thick main root, often 10" (25cm) or more deep, that is the reason this plant is grown.

Originally growing wild in southeastern European coastal areas and the Middle East, it can now also be found abundantly in North America.

You'll find it: Around abandoned and derelict gardens, community gardens, and trash heaps. When in cultivation, it is increased by dividing roots; parts are abandoned and these often colonize areas around gardens. Before digging up roots of plants growing in the wild, the law indicates that you will need permission from the landowner.

Roots: The long, thick, yellow-buff roots have a distinctive and pungent peppery aroma and taste.

Harvesting the roots: Look for plants at the edges of clumps, and use a spade to remove them. Roots in light, sandy soil are much easier to dig up than branching ones in heavy soils. Wash, allow to dry and store in dry sand or peat in a cool dark shed, cellar, or garage. They remain in good condition for several months.

Using the roots: Peel the root, ensuring the brown layer under the surface is removed. This preparation is best undertaken under a running tap or in a bowl of water as it reduces the pungency of the root. The root can then be grated, minced, or crushed and simmered with milk and seasonings to make a peppery sauce to flavor meat, fish, and salads. Horseradish sauce is widely used with roast beef. Freshly grated roots can be used as a garnish for beef or smoked fish, such as mackerel.

MINTS: Peppermint
(*Mentha* x *piperita*)

Also known as: Spanish or Corsican Mint

This hardy herbaceous perennial grows to 18"–30" (30–80cm) high, with masses of lilac-pink to light purple flowers appearing in long, clustered heads during summer. It is a natural hybrid between Water Mint (*M. aquatica*) and Spearmint (*M. spicata*). Peppermint is native to Europe and the Middle East, but is now widely spread throughout many of the world's temperate climates.

You'll find it: Older parts from the plant's center when being divided are often discarded around trash and soil heaps where they establish themselves. Look alongside community gardens and old herb gardens. As an escapee, it is also found in ditches, along roadsides, and in waste grounds.

Leaves: Lance-shaped to oval, hairy, mid-green, and tooth-edged on short stems, the leaves are sometimes reddish green. Leaves have a strong peppermint aroma and flavor.

Harvesting the leaves: Pick young leaves in spring and summer and use as fresh as possible.

Using the leaves: Add sprigs of young leaves to cool summer drinks and to flavor vegetables. The flavor of new potatoes and peas is greatly enhanced by a few sprigs added to the cooking water. Remove the sprigs before serving. When infused, peppermint makes a refreshing tea.

Other Peppermints

The flat and carpeting *M. requienii* is also known as **Peppermint**, as well as being called Spanish Mint, Corsican Mint, and Corsican Thyme. It has round, bright, pale green leaves that when bruised have a distinctive peppermint scent. Throughout the summer it bears long spikes of pale purple flowers and is sometimes grown in combination with Thyme and Chamomile to form a fragrant lawn.

MINTS:
Water Mint
(*Mentha aquatica*)

Another member of the mint family, this strongly scented perennial herb is native throughout Europe, parts of Asia, and Africa. It has spread to North and South America, Australia, and some Atlantic Islands, growing in moist places like swamps and lakes.

Its small lilac flowers are densely crowded into terminal heads and borne on branched, square stems from early summer to early autumn.

You'll find it: Alongside streams, rivers, and ponds, as well as in damp meadows, marshes, and fens, where it grows in clumps about 24" (60cm) high.

Leaves: Somewhat rough-surfaced, oval, hairy, dark green leaves with purple tinges.

Harvesting the leaves: Gather leaves from the top and outside of a clump since these will be more tender and less bitter than more mature leaves.

Using the leaves: Use in the same way as for Peppermint (see page 59) and other mints to make sauces, chutneys, cold drinks, and tea infusions, although you might find the taste slightly bitter. In this case, add sugar to sweeten.

Other Mints to Consider

Apple Mint (*Mentha suaveolens*), sometimes called Woolly Mint, has light green leaves and light purple to pink flowers. It is used to make apple mint jelly and is added to salads and drinks.

Apple Mint

Pineapple Mint (*Mentha suaveolens* 'Variegata') has leaves with creamy-white edges and a pineapple aroma.

Spearmint (*Mentha spicata*), or Common Mint, is a hardy herbaceous, clump-forming perennial that has a large mass of spearmint-flavored leaves. It bears pale purple flowers in dense whorls along branching stems, which grow 18"–24" (45–60cm) high, from mid-summer to early autumn. Native to southern and central Europe, it now grows in temperate climates throughout the world; in many areas, it has escaped from cultivation and into the countryside. It is often found in old and neglected cottage gardens, the edges of community gardens, and country lanes. It is often grown in large containers and pots to constrict growth and prevent its spread.

Pineapple Mint

Spearmint

Mentha **x** *villosa* (also known as *Mentha alopecuroides* and *Mentha nemorosa*) is a cross between Spearmint (*M. spicata*) and Apple Mint (*M. suaveolens*). It grows 12"–24" (30–60cm) high, with square stems and variably colored, occasionally crinkled, tooth-edged, light to mid-green leaves. Small, lavender-violet flowers are borne in whorls in summer. In Cuba, it is known as "Mojito Mint," with slightly citrus-flavored, lightly sweet leaves traditionally used to flavor Mojitos, a famed refreshing punch-like cocktail also popular in North America.

Mentha x villosa

Rosemary
(*Rosmarinus officinalis*)

Native to Mediterranean countries and southern Turkey, this evergreen aromatic shrub now grows in many warm and temperate regions throughout the world and prefers a warm, dry climate. In earlier years, it was especially planted at the fronts of cottages because of a legend that it is the herb of remembrance.

Growing 5'–7' (1.5–2m) high, it spreads and eventually colonizes large areas; its self-sown seeds ensure its spread. During mid- and late spring—and sporadically through to late summer and sometimes into early winter—it bears mauve, tubular flowers with prominent lower lips; the flowers cluster in leaf joints.

You'll find it: Alongside country lanes and near old cottages; additionally, in old and neglected herb gardens and especially where plants were discarded in warm and sheltered corners.

Leaves: Narrow, mid- to dark green, and clustered around stems that are mainly upright; in old plants, they fall sideways and almost rest on the ground.

Harvesting the leaves: Carefully pull off leaves by snapping them sideways; they can be used fresh or dried. To dry them, cut off whole stems and hang them upside down in a cool room. Unfortunately, dried leaves lose some flavor.

Using the leaves: They are used fresh or dried to introduce further flavor to lamb, pork, and veal. Rosemary is also superb for flavoring poultry dishes, roasted vegetables, eggs, fish, sauces, and stuffings.

Uses for Rosemary

- When making roast potatoes, add a scattering of fresh or dried rosemary leaves to the hot oil in your roasting pan. Shake the pan gently to coat the potatoes with the rosemary and oil. Season with salt and roast as normal.
- A sprig of Rosemary in any tomato-based sauce adds a Mediterranean twist.
- It makes a flavorful contribution to minestrone and other vegetable soups and stews.
- Stuff sprigs of Rosemary into the cavity of whole fish or chicken before roasting or barbecuing.

Summer Savory
(*Satureja hortensis*)

Summer savory has an annual nature and forms a mass of young stems, growing 12"–18" (30–45cm) high. It originated in southeastern Europe, but has been spread to many temperate countries, including North America, ranging from Newfoundland south to Virginia, and west to Ohio. Each year, summer savory produces seeds to perpetuate it.

You'll find it: Around old herb gardens and community gardens, especially in disused country gardens. Also look for it on old heaps of soil close to retired herb gardens, where it might have been discarded and formed seed-raised colonies.

Leaves: Spicily flavored, dark green leaves are borne on square, hairy stems. From mid-summer to early autumn, stems become covered in tiny, tubular, lilac flowers that arise from leaf joints.

Harvesting the leaves: Pick young leaves throughout summer and use fresh. Apart from using them soon after being gathered, leaves can be dried for winter use. This is best done by cutting down plants at the end of summer, tying them in bunches, and hanging them upside down in a dry, cool, and airy place. Leaves can be removed as required.

Using the leaves: To flavor fish, meat, soups, cheese and egg dishes, drinks, and stuffings. In southern Europe, summer savory is often used when cooking fava beans.

Winter Savory (*Satureja montana*)

A hardy perennial with a bushy, erect, and woody sub-shrub nature, **Winter Savory** grows up to 12" (30cm) high, sometimes slightly more. From mid-summer to mid-autumn, it bears rose-purple, tubular flowers from the upper leaf joints.

Native to southern Europe and parts of North Africa, it is popular in herb gardens, from where it is often an escapee. In warmer areas it sometimes becomes naturalized on old stone walls.

It has square-sectioned stems bearing gray-green, narrow- or lance-shaped leaves. It is characterized by having a series of small but visible ridges around each stem and between pairs of leaves.

The flavor is considered to be coarser than leaves from Summer Savory (see page 63).

Tansy
(*Tanacetum vulgare*)

Also known as: Bitter Buttons, Common Tansy, Cow Bitter, Garden Tansy, Golden Buttons

A widespread and popular herb with an herbaceous and perennial nature, tansy is native to Europe and Asia, including Siberia, and has been introduced into almost all of North America and countries in the southern hemisphere. It is now naturalized throughout warm and temperate climates, such as South America and Australia along the coasts and in forests.

With its traditional culinary, medicinal, and domestic uses, this cottage-garden perennial was widely grown in herb and kitchen gardens where it created a dominant display of leaves and flowers. It grows to 42" (1m) high, sometimes more.

Popular Strewing Herb

Several centuries ago, many aromatic herbs were scattered on floors of churches, castles, and baronial halls to create a fragrant atmosphere. Tansy, with its distinctive but not particularly appealing scent of chest ointment, was widely used and reputed to keep away flies and to deter lice and fleas. When combined with elder leaves, it was especially protective against flies and moths. However, a more fragrant combination is Tansy leaves, Rosemary, and Thyme.

You'll find it: Old and grassy areas as well as alongside fields, roadsides, hedgerows, country paths, old gardens, and community gardens. It is especially found in areas where old cottages have been demolished or abandoned.

Leaves and flowers: Erect stems bear large, deeply divided, dark green leaves with serrated edges. Bright, golden-yellow, button-like flowers appear in clustered heads from mid- to late summer.

Harvesting the leaves and young shoots: Use a sharp knife to cut off young leaves; old ones are too tough. Also cut off tender young shoots.

Using the leaves and shoots: Young leaves and shoots can be used to flavor omelets; if shredded, they can be added to sandwiches and cheese dishes. Leaves have also been used in traditional puddings and cakes, such as Easter Tansy Pudding. Young leaves were served with fried eggs. Tansy tea was popular and used as a tonic, both as a stimulant and for treating children who had worms.

Wild Garlic
(*Allium ursinum*)

Also known as: Ramsons, Wood Garlic, Bear's Garlic, Buckrams, Devil's Posy, Gypsy Garlic, Hog Garlic, Gypsy Gibbles

A bulbous-based herbaceous perennial with a clump-forming then carpeting nature, it displays umbrella-like heads of 6 to 20 white star-like flowers from mid-spring to early summer, rising above the leaves that grow 20" (50cm) high. Native to large parts of Europe, from Spain to the Caucasus, Scandinavia, central Russia, and southern Turkey, it also flourishes in North America where it was introduced. It thrives in moist woodland.

You'll find it: In damp woods and shady places. Note that it is similar to the poisonous Lily-of-the-Valley before it flowers. Crush a leaf in your fingers to determine which it is—the garlic scent is an indication that you have found an edible plant.

Leaves: Bright green, flat, broadly lance-shaped leaves about 8" (20cm) long are supported on stiff triangular stems and have a distinctive garlic scent.

Harvesting the leaves: Choose young and fresh leaves as these have the best flavor. Although animals usually avoid this plant, it is always best to wash before eating them.

Using the leaves: Although collectively they create a strong garlic aroma, individually and when added to salads their impact is much less. Use as a cooked vegetable or in any recipe calling for garlic; it can also be added to risottos and soups, and makes a very good pesto.

Garlic

In warm regions, especially if the soil is light and well-drained, you might find escapees of the bulbous-based culinary herb **Garlic** (*Allium sativum*), native of Central Asia. Used to flavor many foods, including salads, fish, and meat dishes, it is common in the cuisines of many diverse cultures, from French, Italian, and Polish to Chinese, Thai, and West Indian.

Wild Marjoram
(*Origanum vulgare*)

Also known as: Common Marjoram, Oregano, Organy, Herb Oregano

With a perennial nature, but also spreading by seeds, wild marjoram grows 12"–24" (30–60cm) high, sometimes slightly more. Native to the Mediterranean region, it is now naturalized widely in the temperate Northern Hemisphere, such as most of North America, all of Europe, much of Asia, and northern Africa.

You'll find it: Dry, hilly pastures and banks, alongside roads and paths, and especially where soil is chalky.

Leaves and flowers: Tiny, tubular, rose-purple flowers, borne in densely clustered heads at the tops of stems during mid- and late summer. The round to oval green, gray-tinted leaves are nearly stemless and appear on branched stems.

Harvesting the leaves: Cut off a few sprigs of young leaves, but do not decimate plants.

Using the leaves: Can be used fresh or gently dried slowly in the sun, when they become sweeter. It is an ideal wayside herb for flavoring meat dishes, stews, and casseroles.

Other Marjorams

You might find other marjorams that have escaped from herb gardens.

Knotted Marjoram (*Origanum majorana*), also known as Annual Marjoram and Sweet Marjoram, is a tender perennial growing annually from seeds with a shrubby and bushy nature. Bright green leaves develop from knot-like leaf joints that cluster around red, four-sided stems. Clusters of white, pink, or mauve flowers appear from early to late summer. Young leaves and shoots are used to flavor meat, poultry, and stuffings. Leaves have a stronger flavor when dried and are often used in potpourri. It is also a traditional part of *bouquet garni.*

Knotted Margoram

Pot Marjoram (*Origanum onites*) is a perennial, shrub-like, sprawling plant with bright green, aromatic leaves. It is usually raised annually from seeds and therefore spreads when seeds scatter or plants are discarded at the end of summer. Its branching nature and reddish tinge to the entire plant make it noticeable. Use young leaves, fresh or dried, in stuffings and to flavor meat, poultry, soups, omelets, and sausage meat. It is also popular with veal.

Pot Margoram

Wild Fruits

The strict botanic definition of fruits encompasses nuts as well as the soft and fleshy wayside fruits, such as blackberries, cranberries, and wild strawberries. However, this chapter is devoted to the juicy succulent fruits and the next chapter deals with nuts.

These much-desired fruits are borne on a wide range of plants, from ground-hugging evergreen shrubs to brambles with long, thorny stems and trees, providing fruits such as elderberries, hawthorns, and sloes. Knowing where and when to search for country fruits is a major element in successful foraging, especially as many provide easy pickings for native animals and birds. For each of the fruits in this chapter, the timing and where to find it are clearly indicated, since this is crucial to foraging success.

Do not expect to gather masses of these fruits at one time since, within even a small area, fruits differ in their ripening and picking times. Most are picked and eaten as treats. But when foraging brings in several bowlfuls of the same type of fruit, then jams, jellies, sauces, and pies are possible.

After spending hours searching out and picking wayside fruits, the last thing you want to do is to knock over the container. Always pick fruits into flat-based boxes and regularly tip them into a larger container that has a lid. This way, even if you knock over the picking box, you will not lose your complete harvest. Thoroughly cleaned, large, plastic ice cream containers are ideal when foraging as the lids can be snapped open and closed very easily. They can be labelled with a permanent marker if you are foraging for several different fruits at one time.

If you arrive home from foraging with no telltale signs on your fingers and lips of eating a few (or more) fruits along the way, then you will not have enjoyed yourself to the fullest!

Barberry
(*Berberis vulgaris*)

Also known as: Common Barberry, Jaundice Berry, Pipperidge, Piprage

You might see this thorny, deciduous shrub in old and neglected gardens where it was once grown for its 2"–3" (5–7.5cm) long pendulous clusters of yellow flowers, followed by red berries. It is native to large parts of Europe, northern Africa, and temperate Asia, as well as abundant and now naturalized in North America where it was introduced by early settlers. It grows abundantly in the wild ranging from Nova Scotia to Nebraska, and is cultivated in many countries.

You'll find it: In old gardens, it was traditionally used as a hedging plant, so do not be surprised if you find it around abandoned buildings and alongside roads. Also look for it on waste ground around old dwellings.

Fruits: Red oblong berries, ½" (1cm) long, appear in late summer. These are high in vitamin C and are an important food for small birds. Barberry has also been used to treat liver complaints and jaundice in alternative medicine. However, its very sharp thorns make it quite difficult to pick the fruits in some locations.

 Iranian Delicacy

The dried fruit of barberry is widely used in Iranian cooking—Iran is the world's largest producer of dried Barberry, known as *zereshk* in Persian. *Zereshk* is added to chicken dishes to give a tart flavor; cooked in rice; and made into jams, juices, and fruit rolls in Iran. Try adding a few fresh or dried berries to rice during cooking to give a sharp note to the dish.

Harvesting the fruits: Berries are ripe enough to be picked in autumn when they turn a deep red. Use gloves as the prickly stems can damage your fingers and hands.

Using the fruits: Although acidic, they can be eaten raw and are considered a delicacy in some cultures. However, they are more palatable when candied or preserved in sugar. The fruits make good jams and jellies—use the recipe for Hawthorn Jelly (see page 93) as a template for making Barberry Jelly. In eastern Europe, this jelly is traditionally used to accompany roast meats.

Bilberry
(*Vaccinium myrtillus*)

Also known as: Blaeberry, Crowberry, Whinberry, Whortleberry

Few plants have such delicious fruits as this hardy, deciduous, spreading shrub. Native to large parts of central and northern Europe as well as Greenland, Iceland, western Canada, and the western United States, its appearance belies its value as a foraging plant. Earlier it was widely planted in North America, where it is now established. Its growth is most notable in the southern Rocky Mountains.

Growing 12"–24" (30–60cm) high, it is smothered in oval, slightly pointed and finely tooth-edged, bright green leaves. Drooping, green-pink, rounded flowers are borne singly or in pairs in terminal and side clusters during late spring.

You'll find it: Abundant on mountainsides, in open woodland, and on acid heaths and moors. In windswept areas, you need to search carefully for this plant, as it grows lower than usual.

Fruits: Round, juicy, blue-black, and ¼" (6mm) across. They often cluster under leaves and unless searched out are not easily seen.

Harvesting the fruits: Berries are ready for picking from mid-summer to early autumn.

Using the fruits: Wash before eating. Large fruits are superb with sugar and cream. They make tasty tarts and jams, and can be added to stewed fruits. The dried leaves can be infused in boiling water to make a tea substitute.

Bilberry Tart

There are numerous recipes for bilberry tart but the following one has proved to be popular.

INGREDIENTS

- 1 cup large bilberries
- 4 tablespoons superfine sugar
- 8" (20cm) wide tart tin lined with sweet short-crust pastry. Bake blind to create a base for the berries.
- 4 egg yolks
- 4 tablespoons double cream
- 6 fresh bay leaves

INSTRUCTIONS

1. Wash bilberries.
2. Heat the oven to 350°F (180°C).
3. Mix the sugar and bilberries; tip into the prepared tart case.
4. Beat together the egg yolks and cream, then pour the mixture over the sugared berries.
5. Place bay leaves on top of the tart and bake for 25 minutes or until set. Eat warm or at room temperature.
6. A dollop of cream or vanilla ice cream are delicious companions to this tart!

Blackberry
(*Rubus fruticosus*)

Also known as: Bramble, Brier

Perhaps one of the best-known foraging plants, with lusciously sweet berries in late summer and autumn. The green, prickly, bramble-like leaves assume red-purple shades in autumn. During early and mid-summer, white or pink flowers, about 1" (3mm) wide, appear in clusters. Later, these are the source of the fruits.

Native to Europe (especially southern regions), Mediterranean regions, and Macaronesia (islands in the North Atlantic Ocean, including the Azores, Canary Islands, Cape Verde, and Madeira) but widely naturalized around the temperate regions.

You'll find it: Widespread in hedges and woods, alongside roads and in old, neglected gardens and community gardens, where it forms a tangle of near impenetrable, thorny, arching stems.

Fruits: Color changes from green to red before finally turning rich purple when they are ready for picking.

Harvesting the fruits: Place the fruits in shallow punnets and avoid squashing. Try not to collect more fruits than you can eat; leave some for the wildlife.

Using the fruits: Most fruits are eaten fresh, sometimes with a dusting of sugar and cream, but such is the versatility of blackberries that they are used in a wide range of desserts and jams. They are particularly good with apples in a crumble, in blackberry fool and pancakes, and of course, with vanilla ice cream.

Blackberry Sauce

This is an easy recipe that is excellent with duck, pork, or turkey.

INGREDIENTS
- 1 lb. (450g) blackberries
- 3 tablespoons superfine sugar
- 1 tablespoon lemon juice

INSTRUCTIONS
1. Mix the blackberries, sugar, and lemon juice in a saucepan.
2. Cover and simmer gently for about ten minutes.
3. Remove from the heat, allow to cool slightly, and then blend in a food processer or blender.
4. Strain the mixture to remove seeds and pour into sterilized glass jars. Seal and label the jars when cool.
5. The sauce can be kept in a refrigerator for two or three months, but is best used soon after making.

Blackcurrant
(*Ribes nigrum*)

Also known as: European Black Currant, Squinancy Berry

Widely grown in gardens, it is native to temperate parts of central and northern Europe and northern Asia, but it is cultivated widely throughout the world, including eastern North America and Russia. This hardy clump-forming shrub, up to 5' (1.5m) high, has large, matte green, three- or five-lobed leaves. It bears clusters of drooping, dull purple-green flowers, followed by sprigs of round berries that ripen in the latter part of mid-summer. It grows best in damp, fertile soils.

You'll find it: In moisture-retentive soil in woods and alongside banks.

Fruits: Distinctively black and glossy, but not in such large and dense clusters as cultivated blackcurrants.

Harvesting the fruits: Pick clusters of the fruits, not individual berries. When you get them home, remove individual berries from stems and place in a cool larder rather than the refrigerator since they lose some flavor if excessively chilled.

Using the fruits: Apart from being used fresh with a dusting of sugar and cream, they are made into jams and put in flans and pies. They are also superb in muffins, fools, and as toppings for cheesecake and ice creams. Blackcurrants have been the source of an extremely popular juice and are very high in vitamin C.

 ## Sore Throat Remedy

Blackcurrants have been gathered in the wild for many centuries before the plant began to be cultivated in gardens. The fruits were used in folk medicine to alleviate a sore throat, known as a *quinsy*, and this led to the plant being called Squinancy, an earlier but still relevant common name. Its effectiveness for easing sore throats was vindicated during the Second World War (1939–45) when commercially bottled blackcurrant syrup was given to children suffering from that complaint.

Tea Tricks

Transform a pot of ordinary Indian tea into having the flavor of green tea from China by adding dried blackcurrant leaves to the infusion. When fresh, blackcurrant leaves have a heavy, aromatic aroma, especially when crushed.

Bullace
(*Prunus domestica* subsp. *insititia*)

Also known as: Bullace Plum, Bullums, Bullison, Damson Plum, Green Damson

Closely related to Damsons, the Bullace is sometimes classified as *Prunus insititia*. It is deciduous, brown-barked, and usually forms a densely twiggy and thorny shrub, although it can reach tree-like stature of 6′–15′ (1.8–4.5m) high. Its hairy-surfaced leaves are long, dull, gray-green, and coarsely tooth-edged. It flowers during mid- and late spring, with pear-shaped, broad, pure white petals.

It is a natural hybrid and was widely cultivated in Europe and southwest Asia but later became neglected when improved plum varieties were developed. It was introduced into North America and became known as Bullace Plum and Damson Plum.

You'll find it: Usually near old and abandoned orchards, in hedges, old gardens, and undisturbed corners. It is often found in areas quite remote from houses.

Fruits: Round or shortly oval, drooping fruits are usually blue-black and with a white or purple bloom. They are ¾"–1" (1.8–2.5cm) wide and larger than the fruits of Sloes (see page 107). The stone is bluntly angled, with the fruit's soft flesh clinging to it.

Harvesting the fruits: Although more palatable than the fruits of sloes, their taste is so sharp that they are often left on the shrub or tree until mid- or late autumn. This enables early frosts to soften the flesh and decrease their acidity.

Using the fruits: The range of uses for bullaces is wide, and certainly in earlier years, it was an important culinary fruit in autumn. However, as new varieties of plums, damsons, and gages were introduced, its importance faded. Nevertheless, as a foraging fruit, it is worth seeking with uses ranging from jams and sauces (especially to accompany wood pigeon). Use the recipe for Sloe Gin (see page 108) as a template for making Bullace Vodka, altering with vodka or gin if you prefer.

Cherry Plum
(*Prunus cerasifera*)

Also known as: Myrobalan Plum

This deciduous spreading tree can grow 26' (8m) tall in the wild, but it is mostly found as a scrambling hedgerow plant. It has finely toothed oval, alternate leaves and white flowers with five petals that open before the leaves in early spring. Since it is the first Prunus to flower, it is often confused with Sloe (see page 107).

Native to southeast Europe and the Middle East, it was naturalized in the British Isles and parts of Australia, it now grows abundantly in North America in both temperate and subtropical climates.

You'll find it: Especially alongside hedgerows and thickets on all but the poorest soil. Since it has been widely cultivated, look for it in old and neglected gardens and old orchards. It has also been grown as a decorative shrub and tree.

Fruits: Round 1"–1¼" (2–3cm) across with a stone, the fruits can be either red or yellow. Some foragers claim the taste is a combination of cherry and plum. They can be eaten fresh, but some are quite dry and may need to be transformed into preserves or jellies.

Harvesting the fruits: Ripening from mid-summer to early autumn, try to harvest before the birds get to them. Cut them off and either eat immediately or store in shallow boxes in a well-ventilated room. Use as soon as possible.

Using the fruits: They can be eaten immediately when ripe and on picking. To many tastes they are sharp, but make excellent jams, jellies, and chutney. Try cherry plums in a summer fruit cobbler with other foraged fruits, such as blackberries or raspberries.

Cloudberry
(*Rubus chamaemorus*)

Also known as: Baked Apple, Baked Apple Berry, Malka, Salmonberry, Yellow Berry

Hardy, low-growing, herbaceous perennial, usually only 3"–10" (7.5–25cm) high, depending on the barrenness of the area, with a creeping rootstock that enables it to survive cold regions. Sometimes it has an annual nature and increases itself by seeds each year.

It is native to a wide area of the northern hemisphere, including North America, northern Europe, Scandinavia, and Arctic Russia to central Russia and Germany. Plants flower from early to late summer, with five-petalled white flowers that are highly attractive to flies and bumblebees. Some plants are male, others female; each plant usually has just one flower, with only female plants producing berries.

You'll find it: On open moorland and mountains, and growing among other plants, including heather, cotton grass, and mosses.

Fruits: At first, red and clustering in groups at the tops of stems, they become yellow or amber when ripe during late summer and early autumn. They are often described as small, orange globules packed in heads shaped like a raspberry.

Harvesting the fruits: This needs to be done as soon as the berries ripen, as insects find them tasty. It is a back-breaking task, searching the ground low down and this accounts for the high cost when buying them.

Using the fruits: They are especially tasty when eaten fresh with vanilla ice cream. Foragers new to these berries often find the seeds tough and therefore boil the entire fruits, adding sugar to make jam. This mixture can be reprocessed to make jellies and juices, blended with chocolate ice cream, or made into a refreshing and unique marmalade.

Cowberry
(*Vaccinium vitis-idaea*)

Also known as: Clusterberry, Crowberry, Foxberry, Lingonberry, Mountain Cranberry, Quailberry, Red Whortleberry

This hardy evergreen shrub with creeping roots is native to forests and Arctic tundra throughout the Northern Hemisphere, as well as to areas further south but at high altitudes. It is a popular native plant in North America where it is commercially cultivated in the Pacific Northwest for its berries.

It rarely grows more than 8" (20cm) high, but in places where the weather is congenial, it is slightly more vigorous—up to 12" (30cm). Its dark lustrous green leaves are oval to pear-shaped, tough with serrated edges. Pink or white bell-shaped flowers appear in terminal clusters during late spring and early summer.

You'll find it: On moors and in woods, where the soil is acidic. It is not easy to find, but often forms large, if sparse colonies.

Fruits: Acidic, globular red berries appear from late summer to mid-autumn.

Harvesting the fruits: Gather the berries as soon as they are red—not before. Take care not to squash them and get them home as soon as possible, before they become warm. Place in a cool, airy cupboard, where they can remain for several weeks.

Using the fruits: Often scarcely edible when picked and therefore usually turned into jams and jellies. However, there are other ways to use cowberries: Try them in muffins, baked with apples, or into buns. They can also be cooked with cabbage to give a sharp piquancy to a sometimes dull vegetable. Like cranberries, cowberry jelly is particularly good with turkey, game birds, and venison.

Crab Apple
(*Malus sylvestris*)

Also known as: Crab, Wild Crab Apple, European Apple, Sour Grabs

A native of most of Europe and southwest Asia and, when introduced into North America, became a widespread escapee. It is found growing in the wild in woods containing oak, either individually or in groups. It forms a small tree, up to 25' (7.5m) high, with dull to mid-green leaves, smooth-surfaced, and with bluntly toothed edges. It should not be confused with seedlings from orchard apples, which can be distinguished from the wild crab apple by their downy stems and sweet fruits. During late spring it produces clusters of white flowers flushed with pink.

You'll find it: In hedges, woods, and scrubland.

Fruits: The round, ¾"–1" (1.8–2.5cm) wide fruits are hard, sour tasting, green-yellow, and when ripe, often speckled or flushed with red. Each fruit has a depression at both ends.

Harvesting the fruits: Usually ready in late summer or early autumn. When they turn red, start to fall from the tree or their stems are easily parted from the tree.

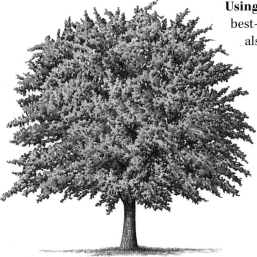

Using the fruits: Crab apple jelly is perhaps the best-known way to use the fruits, but they are also used to make wine, chutney, apple butter, and many jelly variations. Try adding two or three crab apples to ordinary apple tarts or crumbles to introduce a sharp note.

Crab Apple Jelly

INGREDIENTS
- 2 lbs. (900g) crab apples
- Superfine sugar (amount varies based on crab apple juice)
- 2 cloves

INSTRUCTIONS
1. Chop the apples roughly and put into a preserving pan with cloves and enough water to cover.
2. Bring to the boil and simmer until soft and pulpy. Skim foam that arises.
3. Put pulp in muslin layers or a jelly bag to drain overnight, catching the juices in a pan.
4. Discard the pulp and measure the juice. For every 2½ cups (600ml) of juice, add 1 lb. (450g) superfine sugar.
5. Return juice and sugar to the pan and dissolve sugar by heating gently, then boil rapidly for 20 minutes or until setting point is reached.
6. Pour into warm sterilized jars and seal while still warm.

Cranberry
(*Vaccinium oxycoccos*)

Also known as: Bog Berry,
Small Cranberry

You might find this hardy, prostrate, evergreen shrub listed as *Oxycoccus palustris*. It is native to a large area from Europe to Scandinavia, central France, northern Italy, northern Asia to Japan, Greenland, and many parts of North America. It grows widely throughout the cool temperate Northern Hemisphere.

It has wiry stems and small, oval, pointed, dark green leaves (whitish below); long stems often develop roots that help secure the plant in the ground. Pink flowers, with four spreading or turned-down petals, appear from early to late summer, with the fruits in autumn.

You'll find it: In bogs and wet heaths, but you may need to search for it under other shrubs.

Fruits: Round or slightly oval red berries appear from late summer to mid-autumn. Sometimes, they have small, brown spots. The berries are borne individually at the ends of thin stems, which arise from leaf joints along main stems.

Harvesting the fruits: Pick the berries individually when richly colored. Usually, you will not be able to find sufficient berries to make a pie; they are best used to make sauces.

Using the fruits: When picked they have a tart, acidic flavor. To many people's taste, they are almost inedible when uncooked. Cranberries are at their best when used to make traditional sauces to accompany turkey or venison.

North American Introduction

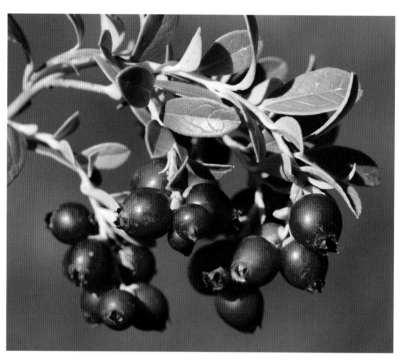

Known as the **Large Cranberry** or American Cranberry, *Vaccinium macrocarpon* (earlier listed as *Oxycoccus macrocarpos*), is native to North America as well as being introduced into other countries. It has been cultivated in its native countries and Europe for its large berries. It is now ideal for foraging in commercially abandoned areas, and the berries mix very well with smaller-berried species.

Dewberry
(*Rubus caesius*)

Also known as: Token Berry,
European Dewberry

A popular wild bramble with slender, prickly, sprawling stems. Due to its low, deciduous nature, it is often unnoticed, especially as it does not produce many fruits during some seasons. This reluctance to bear fruits has encouraged its country name Token Berry. It rarely grows beyond 16" (40cm) high. The leaves have three green leaflets and are slightly hairy on both sides.

Clusters of white, five-petalled flowers appear from early summer to early autumn and are followed by the distinctive fruits. Dewberry is common in many areas, particularly along coastal regions in Europe from Scandinavia to Spain, Greece and Sicily, and also in Asia and Russia. It is naturalized sparingly in Argentina, Canada, and the United States.

You'll find it: Along roadsides, coastal regions, in scrub and dry grassland, and especially in chalky areas. It tends to grow well among Blackberries (see page 76).

Fruits: They are different from other bramble fruits in being formed of fewer but larger drupelets (individually they form the characteristic clustered shape of fruits in the bramble family). When ripe they are bluish, with a distinctive white bloom.

Dewberry plants often grow in the same areas as blackberries, but they flower earlier, and the fruits can be readily identified by their shape and early appearance.

Harvesting the fruits: The fruits are ready for picking from mid-summer to autumn. At this stage they are soft, juicy, and easily squashed. For this reason, cut them off in clusters, with a small stem intact and attached to them.

Using the fruits: There are never enough fruits to meet the demand, so view dewberries as "treats." Eat as you pick, or if you manage to get them home, dip using their stems into bowls of cream and sugar.

Elderberry
(*Sambucus nigra*)

Also known as: Bour Tree, Common Elder, European Elder

This deciduous shrub or tree, up to 30' (9m) high, is best known for its fragrant flowers and for the dark purple-red fruits. Native to wide areas of Europe, southwest Asia, and northern Africa, it often grows where little else thrives. It is common throughout the British Isles, and introduced to most parts of the world, including North America.

Sweet-smelling, creamy-white flowers appear in large, flat heads up to 8" (20cm) wide in early summer. The matte green leaves, usually formed of five leaflets, have an acrid aroma when young.

You'll find it: Abundant in woods, waste grounds, and hedgerows, especially where soil is fertile and moisture retentive.

Fruits: Round berries, first green, then purple-black and ¼" (6mm) wide when ripe, appear in late summer and early autumn.

Harvesting the flowers and fruits: Cut flowers off in clusters. Before using the flowers, check that they are free from insects—shake but don't wash. When ripe, cut off berries in clusters with a small piece of stem still attached.

Using the fruits and flowers: Elderberry wine can be made from the ripe fruits, while the flowers yield that great summer favorite, Elderflower Cordial. The fresh flowerheads can also be dipped in a sweet batter and turned into fritters.

Elderflower Cordial

INGREDIENTS
- 7½ cups (1.5kg) sugar
- 5 cups (1.2 L) water
- 20 elderflower heads
- 2 lemons
- ⅓ cup (75g) citric acid

INSTRUCTIONS
1. Dissolve the sugar and water in a pan and bring to the boil.
2. Place the flowers in a large bowl.
3. Pare the lemons in wide strips and slice the lemons. Add peel and slices to bowl.
4. Pour the boiling syrup over the bowl ingredients, stir in the citric acid to dissolve, then cover and let stand overnight. Citric acid is available in most grocery stores or pharmacies.
5. Strain cordial through muslin cloth and place in sterilized screw-top jars or bottles.
6. To use, dilute the cordial with either still or sparkling water.

Gooseberry
(*Ribes uva-crispa*)

Also known as: English Gooseberry, European Gooseberry, Goosegog

Earlier known as *Ribes grossularia*, this deciduous, spiny, much-branched shrub is native to a wide area, including southern Europe, Scandinavia, and North Africa. It is also established in North America, where it has escaped from cultivation. It grows most abundantly in Europe's hedges and woodlands, often on the banks of rivers or streams.

Bushes grow about 42" (1m) high, with three- or five-lobed, matte green leaves and clusters of small, green to pink-green flowers with purple tinges during late spring and early summer.

You'll find it: Indigenous plants are most often seen in shaded, moisture-retentive areas alongside streams, but escapees from cultivation are found mainly alongside hedges and in woods where they have been spread by birds eating the fruits and scattering seeds.

Fruits: Usually hairy, round or oval, green, yellow-green or red-purple fruits in mid- and late summer borne in small, drooping clusters.

Harvesting the fruits: Pick the berries individually as they ripen, leaving the short stem intact with the fruit. Do not just tear them off the bush. Take care that thorns on the bush do not damage your fingers.

Using the fruits: Unripe fruits are sometimes picked early and used with Fennel (see page 56) in a sauce to accompany mackerel. Most fruits, however, are picked when ripe and eaten fresh with a dusting of sugar and cream. They are also ideal in preserves.

Gooseberry Fool

As a dessert, gooseberry fool has few rivals and is very easy to make.

INGREDIENTS

- 12 oz. (350g) gooseberries
- ½ cup (85g) sugar (or to taste)
- 1½ cups (350ml) cold custard (or a mix of custard and whipped cream)

INSTRUCTIONS

1. Wash the fruits. Top and tail to remove ends and stems.
2. Simmer gooseberries in a dash of water and sugar for a short time until pulpy and hot.
3. Purée the gooseberries in a food processor and seive, or simply crush with a wooden spoon.
4. Allow the purée to cool before folding it into cold custard for a delightful summer treat.
5. If you have more or less fruit to start with, then alter the quantities to fit your own situation.

Hawthorn
(*Crataegus monogyna*)

Also known as: Common Hawthorn, English Hawthorn, May-bush, May-tree, Whitethorn, May

A widely seen, spiny-branched, deciduous shrub or small tree up to 30' (9m) high with shiny, dark green, deeply lobed leaves appearing in mid-spring. These are followed in late spring and early summer by white (sometimes pink), heavily scented flowers borne in dense, flattened clusters. Hawthorn is native to Europe, northwestern Africa, and the Middle East, but has been introduced to many other countries worldwide. Apart from Europe, it can be found along the coasts of North America, as well as northern and southern Africa.

You'll find it: In woods and open land, on scrub land, and in country hedges, where it has been planted for hundreds of years. Found on most soils, other than excessively wet land, fens, and bogs.

Fruits: Often known as haws, the deep red round fruits appear in autumn.

Harvesting the fruits: The fruits, when glossy and fully ripe, are best picked in a cluster, taking care to avoid the prickles. Remove individually from the group and wash and dry them.

Using the fruits and leaves: Young leaves have a surprisingly nutty flavor and are sometimes added to early salads or sandwiches. When fully ripe, the vitamin C–rich fruits are said to have a slight flavor of avocado pears and are often made into jellies to add sharpness to cheese and other savory dishes.

Hawthorn Jelly

Gather the ripe red haws before birds take them.

INGREDIENTS

- 1 lb. 9 oz. (700g) hawthorn fruit
- 2 cups (430ml) water
- Superfine sugar (amount varies based on hawthorn juice)
- 1 lemon, juiced

INSTRUCTIONS

1. Remove the haws, wash, dry, and ensure the stems have been taken off.
2. Put the fruit in a heavy saucepan and add water. Bring to the boil and simmer for an hour. Mash the berries every 20 minutes with a potato masher.
3. Put the mixture in a muslin bag and allow to drain overnight. Do not squeeze the mixture.
4. Place in a clean saucepan. For every 2½ cups (600ml) of the juice, add l lb. (450g) of superfine sugar. Also add the juice of a lemon.
5. Slowly dissolve the sugar and boil for 10 minutes.
6. Remove surface foam. Once the setting point has been reached, pour into sterilized, warm jars with screw lids. Store in a cool dark place.

Hop
(*Humulus lupulus*)

Also known as: Bine, Common Hop, European Hop

This distinctive perennial herbaceous climber sends up fresh shoots each year that spread 10'–15' (3–4.5m) over supports or nearby plants. Twining stems (known as bines) bear deeply cut, three- or five-lobed hairy leaves up to 6" (15cm) wide. Pale yellow-green cones (the female parts) are borne in groups of two or three from leaf joints during mid- and late summer, and sometimes slightly later.

These cones have been used to brew beer for more than 500 years, providing flavor and stabilizing the brew. The small male flowers are much less distinctive and are normally borne on separate plants.

It is native to Europe, the Middle East, and North America, but is widely distributed as an escapee from cultivation. It grows best in full sun with moderate rainfall, and can be found growing wild in the northern United States, eastern Canada, Australia, and Morocco.

You'll find it: In hedges and thickets, along the edges of farmland, or escapees from hop gardens where it was raised abundantly for its part in making beer. It is prevalent in fertile, moisture-retentive soils.

Fruits: These are the hops, which look like inverted cones, about ¾" (1.8cm) long, sometimes more.

Harvesting the fruits: Pick the hops individually, taking care not to crush them.

Using the young shoots: Young shoots can be cut out in spring, chopped up, and boiled as a vegetable. Alternatively, simmer in butter and add to omelets. A further variation is to cut a handful of young shoots, arrange the cut ends together, tie loosely, and immerse in salted water for about an hour. Then wash and plunge into boiling water until tender, usually only a few minutes. Serve drizzled with melted butter or olive oil as a side dish.

Hottentot Fig
(*Carpobrotus edulus*)

Also known as: Highway
Ice Plant, Sour Fig

You might find this creeping, drought-resistant perennial from South Africa also listed as *Mesembryanthemum edule*. It is mostly found growing on coastal and inland slopes in South Africa, ranging from the Northern, Western, and Eastern Capes.

Trailing rooting underground stems produce mats of narrow, upwardly curved thick, triangular-shaped green moisture-retentive leaves up to 4" (10cm) long. The magenta or yellow flowers are about 2" (5cm) across and appear during early and mid-summer. In warm countries, flowers often develop earlier, and this brings forward the time when fruits appear.

You'll find it: In sandy ground, banks, loose sand dunes, and gravely lime-rich gardens. Its coastal spread is partly due to gulls pulling up stems and later dropping them, where they develop roots and produce further colonies.

Fruits: In late summer fleshy, edible, reddish, fig-shaped fruits, about 1½" (3.5cm) in diameter and shaped like a spinning top.

Harvesting the fruits: Cut off the fruits when they become fragrant and color is intense. If left, the fruit becomes tough, leathery, and wrinkled.

Using the fruits: Can be eaten fresh but have a strongly sour taste. When able to ripen in full sun for several weeks, the fruits are used to make a tart jam.

 ## Ecology Warning

In coastal areas in some countries, it has been used to stabilize sand dunes and gravelly soil, where it grows rapidly, stabilizes, and assumes command of large areas, to the detriment of indigenous plants. Additionally, where black rats are prevalent, the hottentot fig provides further food for them, and rats spread the plant further through their faeces.

Juniper
(*Juniperus communis*)

Also known as: Bastard Killer, Common Juniper, Juniper Berry, Juniper Fruit

This hardy, evergreen, shrub-like conifer, but sometimes a tree 20' (6m) or more high, has a prickly nature. The needle-like, sharply pointed, grayish leaves, each with a broad white band on its upper surface, have an apple-like fragrance when crushed.

It is found in wide areas, in northern temperate regions, and northward to the Arctic Circle where it reveals itself as a dwarf species; also in the mountains of North Africa and the Himalayas, as well as in North America in northern California and Pennsylvania.

You'll find it: An abundant and widespread conifer, native to heaths, moors, pine woods, and birch woods, and especially dominant on chalk downs and limestone hills.

Caution for Mothers

Gin, which contains juniper as a flavoring, was known in the 18th and 19th centuries as Mother's Ruin. The effects of eating juniper could be dangerous for pregnant women or the baby. Nowadays, pregnant women, those wishing to become pregnant, and nursing mothers should take care not to eat the berries or drink extracts from juniper.

Fruits: The round or slightly oval female fruits, about ¼" (6mm) across, appear during early summer; in the first year, they are green. In the latter part of their second year, usually during late summer and into autumn, they become black and covered with a blue bloom. Each fruit encloses two or three seeds in a resinous, mealy pulp. The small yellow cones are male and are borne on separate plants.

Harvesting the fruits: When gathering ripe berries, wear gloves to protect your hands from the prickly foliage.

Using the fruits: Mostly associated with gin, juniper berries have several other culinary uses. Crushed juniper berries, whether fresh or dried, are ideal in marinades for meats, and they are excellent added to pork, goose, and beef dishes. Wild game, especially venison, is another great partner to this useful flavoring.

Medlar
(*Mespilus germanica*)

A deciduous tree, the medlar is densely twigged, often has a crooked appearance, thickly clad in thorns, and usually under 20' (6m) high. Distinctively, it forms a spreading canopy of dull green crinkled, finely tooth-edged, lance-like leaves up to 5" (13cm) long.

Five-petalled, 2" (5cm) wide, saucer-shaped flowers appear at the ends of short, young shoots in the latter part of mid-spring and until early summer, followed by apple-shaped fruits.

It is native to the southeastern part of the Balkan peninsula and southwest Asia. However, it is also found in southeastern Europe, especially the Black Sea coasts of Bulgaria and Turkey, as well as parts of North America. It needs temperate and Mediterranean climate conditions in order to thrive.

You'll find it: Around old and neglected gardens and in orchards in warm areas. Also look for it in ancient hedges and among brambles.

Fruit: Round green fruits that resemble very large rose hips; each has a distinctive five-tailed calyx that partly encapsulates the fruit.

Harvesting the fruits: In warm countries, fruits can be eaten from the tree, but in cool climates, fruits do not become palatable until half-rotten, sometimes known as "bletted." At this stage, they become soft and brown. In temperate climates, harvest when the weather is dry in late autumn. Place in slatted trays in a frost-proof shed or room until they are ripe (soft and brown) and ready for eating or making into preserves.

Using the fruits: Scrape the brown interior flesh from the skin; eat with a dusting of sugar and cream. Medlar jelly is a popular accompaniment for lamb and game. The jelly is also good on scones or toast.

Medlar Jelly

Use soft ripened fruits to make jelly.

1. Boil medlars in a small amount of water until pulpy, then strain through a jelly bag or muslin cloth.
2. Simmer strained juice with preserving sugar (2½ cups [500g] to each 2¼ cups [500ml] fruit juice) and a squeeze or two of lemon juice until it reaches setting point.
3. Place in sterilized jars once it has cooled, cover, and store in a cool dark cupboard.

Mountain Ash
(*Sorbus aucuparia*)

Also known as: Common Rowan, European Mountain Ash, Quickbeam, Rowan, Rowan Tree, Wicken-tree

Mountain ash is a slender and erect deciduous tree that develops a spreading nature with age, usually 20' (6m) high. The 5"–9" (13–23cm) mid-green leaves are formed of six or seven pairs of narrow leaflets. Clusters of white flowers in flattish heads appear during early and mid-summer. It is native to much of Europe and Asia, as well as Morocco. It was introduced to North America, where it has become widespread from plains to mountains up to the tree line, from Washington to Alaska and eastward in Canada.

You'll find it: In woods, scrubland, and on mountainsides. It is more prevalent in areas with light or slightly acid soil. It can be found as an escapee in fields and hedges.

Fruits: Large clusters of round or slightly oval fruits ripen to a rich scarlet or bright red from early to late autumn.

Harvesting the fruits: Pick entire clusters of fruits when ripe but before they become soft and mushy.

Using the fruits: The fruits are most commonly used in jelly to accompany game and lamb. They can also be used in combination with crab apples to make jelly (see page 100).

Mountain Ash and Crab Apple Jelly

1. Remove stems from the Rowan fruits and wash. Wash the crab apples and cut away bruised and pest-infested parts.
2. Place in a heavy-based saucepan, cover with water, and simmer until tender.
3. Strain the mixture through a muslin bag but do not squeeze. Let all the moisture drain through naturally to avoid clouding the jelly.
4. Warm the sugar before putting it into the liquid. For every 2¼ cups (500ml) of the liquid, measure 2½ cups (500g) preserving sugar into an ovenproof dish. Place in a moderate oven for 10–15 minutes.
5. Put the warmed sugar and strained juice into a saucepan, stir until dissolved, bring to the boil, then simmer until it reaches setting point.
6. Skim the surface to remove the froth, and allow to cool slightly.
7. While still warm, pour into sterilized jars.

Oregon Grape
(*Mahonia aquifolium*)

Also known as: Blue Barberry, Holly Barberry, Holly Grape, Holly-leaved Barberry, Mountain Grape

A distinctive, hardy, suckering evergreen shrub that grows up to 5' (1.5m) high and slowly spreads to form sprawling colonies. Its holly-like leaves are tough, leathery, glossy, and dark green, up to 12" (30cm) long and each formed of five to nine leaflets. During mid- and late spring, it develops richly fragrant, golden-yellow flowers in clustered heads 3"–5" (7.5–13cm) across. These are followed in early autumn by masses of berries.

Native to North America, from British Columbia to northern California, it was widely planted in Europe and other countries to provide cover and food for pheasants. It has spread and become naturalized in many areas. It is most common in western North America, as well as in the Cascades, Rockies, and northern Sierra Nevada.

You'll find it: As an escapee around old and neglected gardens, alongside fields, and on moors, especially where the soil is moisture retentive.

Fruits: During early autumn, plants become covered in clusters of round black berries, slightly more than ¼" (6mm) across and with a violet bloom. They often appear like miniature grapes, and this has encouraged some of its popular common names, such as Oregon Grape, Mountain Grape, and Holly Grape.

Harvesting the fruits: Pick them in clusters as soon as they are ripe and starting to soften.

Using the fruits: High in vitamin C, they can be eaten fresh from the plant, although for some tastes they are tart and best eaten with a dusting of sugar and cream. Alternatively, the fruits can be made into a jelly to accompany meat, especially venison and pork. Berries can be crushed and fermented to produce a wine, but needs a high proportion of sugar to counteract the acidity of the brew.

Raspberry
(*Rubus idaeus*)

Also known as: European
Raspberry, Framboise, Hindberry,
Red Raspberry, Wild Raspberry

Raspberry bushes or canes have a suckering, scrambling, and sprawling nature with unbranched stems about 5' (1.5m) long, armored with slender, straight prickles. The green leaves are formed of several oval, coarsely tooth-edged leaflets, 1½"–4" (3.5–10cm) long. Clusters of small pinkish flowers appear in clusters at the ends of short twigs that arise on one-year-old stems from early to late summer. Later, these produce the succulent fruits.

It is native to wide areas, from much of Europe to Iceland, into Russia, and abundant throughout Asia and much of North America. It is commonly cultivated in temperate regions.

You'll find it: In woods and hedgerows, on heaths and especially in hilly areas. It is also a bold escapee and becomes established in hedges, old gardens, and community gardens. It is spread by birds eating the fruits, so expect to find it over a wide area.

Fruits: Ripen to red (only rarely to yellow) from mid-summer to early autumn. Each fruit is formed of several drupelets.

Harvesting the fruits: Pick as soon fully red and readily part from the stem. Treat carefully as they squash easily, especially when overripe.

Using the fruits: They are best eaten fresh, but raspberries can be used in hundreds of ways—in cakes, summer puddings, with meringues, fools, and in sauces to accompany ice cream. Chocolate and raspberry are a favorite combination.

Eton Mess

This simple combination of raspberries, broken meringues, and whipped cream make the most of foraged summer fruits.

1. Pick over a punnet of foraged raspberries to remove leaves, stems, and the odd insect.
2. Reserving a few raspberries for decoration, add a sprinkling of sugar to the rest of the raspberries and crush with the back of a fork.
3. Break up several meringues, then fold whipping cream, crushed berries, and meringues together gently.
4. Divide into serving dishes and top with a few berries.

Redcurrant
(*Ribes rubrum*)

Also known as: Northern Redcurrant, Wineberry

This spreading deciduous shrub, up to 5' (1.5m) high, has three- or five-lobed green leaves, often with heart-shaped bases. Unlike blackcurrant, which is clump-forming and with many stems arising from ground level, redcurrant often has just one main stem, with branches growing from it. During mid- and late spring, it develops clusters of saucer-shaped, drooping, greenish flowers from leaf joints on the previous season's stems. It is from these flowers that the fruits develop.

Earlier known as *Ribes sativum*, it is native to western Europe and Asia and spreading into Scandinavia and Russia. It is also found in North America and has become naturalized in many other countries.

You'll find it: In woods and along hedgerows, where the soil drains well but is moisture retentive. It also grows in damp rocky places and mountain woods.

Fruits: Although it does not fruit as heavily as Blackcurrant (see page 78), the red, juicy, sweet, shining berries have few rivals in taste and visual appeal. They ripen during mid-summer.

Harvesting the fruits: Wait until the fruits are fully ripe, then snip them off in clusters.

Using the fruits: Like many other types of currants, they are best eaten fresh with a dusting of sugar. Tarts, jams, jellies, and syrups are other options, as well as making redcurrant sauce. Redcurrants are also a mainstay of a British favorite, summer pudding.

Redcurrant Sauce

INGREDIENTS

- 1 lb. (450g) redcurrants
- 1⅓ cups (300g) soft brown sugar
- 2 orange peel pieces
- 1 shallot, finely chopped
- 2 sprigs rosemary
- Small wineglass of port

INSTRUCTIONS

1. Place all the ingredients in a heavy-based saucepan or a preserving pan. Heat to a simmer for about 20 minutes, until it becomes sticky and resembles a slightly runny jam.
2. Pick out the rosemary and pieces of orange peel. Leave the mixture to cool slightly.
3. Before cool, put in clean, sterilized jars and label. Store in a cool dark cupboard and eat with lamb and other roasted meats.

Service Tree
(*Sorbus torminalis*)

Also known as: Wild Service Tree, Chequers Tree, Checkers Tree, Chokers Tree

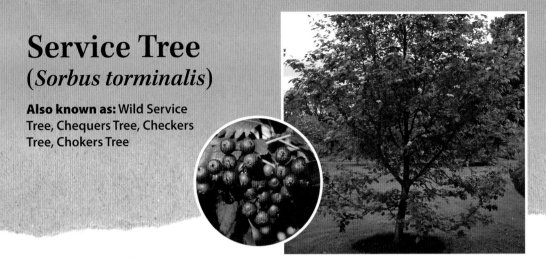

A deciduous tree mostly found in ancient woodlands and hedgerows, it grows to 65' (20m) high and can be 50' (15m) wide, with dark brown to pale gray bark. Its leaves are dark green with three to five pairs of toothed, pointed lobes, much like a maple leaf. The white five-petalled flowers are borne in loose, branched clusters in late spring or early summer. It is native to Europe, northwestern Africa, and Asia, as well as growing in North America as an introduced plant. It is most likely to be found in Britain's woodland.

You'll find it: In woods, particularly those with oak and ash and in hedgerows. It prefers clay and lime-based soils.

Fruits: Shaped like small apples or pears and ½"–¾" (1.2–1.8cm) long, greenish to russet or brown and speckled with rusty lenticels. The fruits are sometimes known as "chequers."

Harvesting the fruits: They can be hard, sour, and bitter if gathered too soon; wait until mid- to late autumn, but still allow for a period of bletting so that the fruits become almost overripe. Once they reach this stage, they become edible and very sweet.

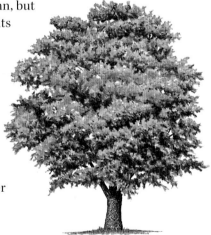

Using the fruits: Once bletted, the fruits are excellent both raw and cooked. When eaten raw, their taste has been likened to that of plum brandy with overtones of dried apricot. They can also be used in preserves and jellies. In earlier times, before the widespread availability of hops, they were used to flavor beer and to make an alcoholic beverage.

Sloe
(*Prunus spinosa*)

Also known as: Blackthorn, Hedge Picks, Wild Plum of Western Europe

A well-known deciduous shrub or small tree, 10'–15' (4–4.5m) high, with rigid stems and a much-branched nature, it often forms a dense thicket of shoots and spines. Dull green, oval leaves 1¾" (4cm) long cluster at the ends of spine-clad stems, with small, pure white flowers appearing singly or in pairs in early or mid-spring on naked stems before the leaves develop.

Originally native to Europe, the Middle East, and northwest Africa, it is now naturalized in New Zealand, Tasmania, and in the United States's Pacific Northwest and New England regions.

You'll find it: In hedgerows, open woods, and scrubland, often growing in poor soil, although it does demand plenty of sunshine.

Fruits: Are round and about ½" (1cm) across. Blue at first, but when ripe, a beautiful shiny black and often have a slight bloom.

Harvesting the fruits: Pick when ripe in mid-autumn; pull off, complete with their small stems. At this stage, they are tart and acidic. Place in trays and put in a cool place indoors.

Using the fruits: The fruit's main claim to fame is in delicious Sloe Gin, for which there are many recipes.

Sloe Gin

INGREDIENTS

- Sloes
- Sugar (¼ the weight of the sloes)
- Almond essence
- 1 small cinnamon stick

INSTRUCTIONS

1. Wash the ripe sloes, dry, and prick with a sharp knife or fork.
2. Half-fill a large, wide-necked (but sealable) sterilized jar or bottle with fruits. Add sugar and top up with gin.
3. Add a drop or two of almond essence and cinnamon stick.
4. Seal the jar, then shake to mix the sugar and gin with the sloes; place in a cool, dark cupboard. Repeat the mixing daily for two or three weeks. Then allow to stand undisturbed for three or four months.
5. Pour off the juice, which should be a deep, ruby red. It can now be drunk in modest amounts. Place the sloe gin in a screw-capped bottle.
6. The fruits will be soft, edible, and steeped in gin, so take care! Try a few with ice cream.

Whitebeam
(*Sorbus aria*)

Also known as: Chess Apple, Hen Apple, Whitten, Whittenbeam

This deciduous tree, occasionally a shrub, is usually 25'–30' (7.5–9m) high, sometimes more. It forms a dense crown of branches that become smothered with oval, occasionally pear-shaped, green leaves up to 4" (10cm) long and coated on their undersides in a dense, white felt. During late spring and early summer, it develops 2"–3" (5–7.5cm) wide clustered heads of dull-white flowers, each about ½" (1cm) wide.

It is native throughout central and southern Europe, including southern Spain, Italy, and Corsica. It has been planted as a decorative tree in many countries, including North America, northern Africa, and temperate Asia.

You'll find it: In woods and scrubland on chalk and in limestone soils. It is spread by birds eating the fruits, so look for it on the fringes of woods as well as in more open sites, and especially in suburbs of towns where it has been planted as a street tree.

Fruits: The oval or round fruits, about ½" (1cm) long, appear in late summer and ripen to scarlet red in autumn.

Harvesting the fruits: Cut them from the tree in bunched clusters when most of the fruits are richly ripe; place in trays in a cool room.

Using the fruits: Like several other fruits, when newly harvested they are inedible and best left until bletted. To do this, store in trays in a cool, dry place until they are almost going rotten. It is only at this stage that they are edible and have acquired the flavor of luscious tropical fruits. They can be made into a jelly on their own or mixed with rose hips. Additionally, when harvested, fruits can be slowly dried in a slightly warm oven, then ground into a powder, and mixed with a cereal, such as wheat.

Wild Cherry
(*Prunus avium*)

Also known as: Bird Cherry, Brandy Mazzard, Crab Cherry, Gean, Massard, Mazzard, Sweet Cherry

A lofty deciduous tree, the wild cherry grows up to 60' (18m) high, open-branched, with shiny, smooth, red-brown peeling bark. The oval, light dull-green leaves usually have a drawn-out point and are 3"–5" (7.5–13cm) long. Pure white, five-petalled, slightly cup-shaped flowers are borne in clusters during mid- and late spring.

Native and widespread across Europe and western Asia, as well as in the mountains of northern Africa, it was introduced to North America, where it has become established and spread across the northern United States and Canada.

You'll find it: In woods and hedges, alongside orchards and farmland and especially where the soil is fertile.

Fruits: The sweet or tart, rich black-red, cherry-like fruits ripen in mid-summer and hang in clusters from short spurs that previously produced the flowers. Birds are quickly attracted to them, and this is the main way that the tree spreads.

Harvesting the fruits: Pick the cherries as soon as they ripen, preferably with their stems still attached.

Using the fruits: Sweet cherries are best eaten fresh, as soon as picked. They are also delicious poached with a bit of sugar and make an excellent pie filling or cobbler. Those with a bitter taste are better used to create cherry brandy.

Cherry Brandy

There are many recipes for making cherry brandy. This one is simple.

1. Remove stems from the cherries, then wash and allow them to dry. Prick each cherry several times to encourage the absorption of brandy.
2. Fill a clean, wide-necked, sterilized bottle that can be sealed with a lid to ¾ full with cherries.
3. Add a couple of tablespoons of sugar, depending on the sweetness of the cherries.
4. Fill the bottle to the top with cheap brandy, seal the bottle or jar, and shake thoroughly.
5. Leave in a cool, dark cupboard until late December, where a tasty and alcoholic treat awaits you.

Wild Rose
(*Rosa canina*)

Also known as: Briar Rose, Brier Rose, Dog Berries, Dog Briar, Dog Brier, Dog Rose, Wild Dog Rose

With its long arching stems, up to 10' (3m) long and packed with curved or hooked prickles, the wild rose provides a formidable fortress for the flowers and fruits. The dull green leaves are formed of five to seven broadly oval leaflets, each up to 1½" (3.5cm) long. During early and mid-summer, white or pinkish, sweetly scented, five-petalled flowers are borne singly or in small clusters along the stems.

Native to Europe, northern Africa, and the Middle East, it is widespread and common, but has also been introduced to many other countries, and is now commonly planted in landscapes across the United States and Canada. The wild rose has been used as rootstock for varieties of cultivated roses, and from that role has spread and become naturalized in many areas.

You'll find it: In hedges, scrubland, and woods, where it usually entangles itself with other plants and produces a wide clump of prickly stems.

Fruits: Known as Rose Hips and occasionally Pixie Ears, Dog Berries, and Dog Hips, the round or egg-shaped fruits ripen to a rich bright red.

Harvesting the fruits and flowers: Gather the petals when one or two have dropped from the flowers, and use soon after. Fruits are gathered when richly colored in autumn, preferably after the first frost.

Using the fruits and flowers: Petals can be used in salads, jams, rose-petal jelly, Turkish delight, and rose vinegar. The fruits are famed in preserves, syrups, and jellies. They are rich in vitamin C; during times of hardship and scarcity of other fruits, they have been made into rose hip syrup that was given to children to keep colds at bay.

Wild Strawberry
(*Fragaria vesca*)

Also known as: Sow-teat's Strawberry, Woodland Strawberry

A perennial plant with a thick, woody base producing long runners that develop roots at their leaf joints, its leaves are usually formed of three oval and coarsely serrated leaflets, bright green above and pale green beneath. White five-petalled flowers with deep yellow centers, up to ¾" (1.8cm) across, appear on short stems from mid-spring to mid-summer.

It is native to southern Europe, North America, Madeira, Azores, and much of Asia. It has also been planted in warm and temperate regions from where it has escaped into the countryside.

You'll find it: In woods, grassland, and scrubland, especially where the soil is fertile and slightly chalky.

Fruits: Small, intensely flavored fruits, about ½" (1cm) across and usually red, they have a sublime flavor compared with commercial berries.

Harvesting the fruits: Pick as soon as they are red, usually in late summer. If left on the plant too long they quickly deteriorate.

Using the fruits: Best eaten fresh, either on their own or with cream. They are usually sweet enough not to require a dusting of sugar.

Cava and Wild Strawberry Jellies

Cava is a sparkling wine similar to Champagne. Make the most of a handful of delicious wild berries in this summery jelly.

INGREDIENTS
- 4 gelatin sheets
- 1 bottle Cava, chilled
- 1 tablespoon sugar

INSTRUCTIONS
1. Set ½ cup (100ml) of Cava aside to warm to room temperature.
2. Soak gelatin sheets in cold water for 5 minutes. Squeeze out excess water.
3. Add room-temperature Cava to a small bowl over a pan of water. Add the gelatin and sugar. Heat through.
4. Remove from the heat, and add 1 cup (250ml) cold Cava. Stir.
5. Place a few berries in the base of four wine glasses or other pretty dessert dishes.
6. Pour over the gelatin-Cava mixture, then refrigerate until set.
7. Garnish with a few more berries if you have any left.

Wild Nuts

Botanical definitions of nuts can be confusing. Here, it is used in its popular sense for any seed or fruit enclosed in a hard or brittle shell. Trees are the main source for these nuts, which are mainly harvested in autumn and range from acorns to walnuts. Rich in protein, fats, and oils, nuts are a nutritious and healthy addition to a modern diet and certainly provided our forebears with valuable calories. For example, 1 lb. (450g) of walnuts provides about 3,000 calories, while beech mast (nuts of the beech tree) yields up to 20 percent of its volume in an oil that is rich in minerals, vitamins, and proteins.

Nuts quickly provide foragers with large amounts of nutritious food, but these nuts are often an essential part of stored food for wild animals, enabling them to survive throughout winter; therefore, do not strip trees bare of nuts.

After harvesting nuts, keep dry; they decay quickly if damp and placed in a cupboard with little air circulation. When nuts are collected while still damp—perhaps after a few weeks of continuous rain—they need to be dried in slight warmth in a well-ventilated place before being stored for use in late autumn or winter.

For many early peoples throughout the world, long before wheat and barley were domesticated, nuts like acorns were a major source of food. Apart from feeding early people, acorns were a central food for the animals they hunted, including deer, wild turkeys, squirrels, and wild fowl. In many areas, the challenge to eat and survive was met by acorns—a simple and unprepossessing nut.

This chapter describes five sources of nuts for foragers in temperate climates, but there are many others in warm climates, including Australian native plants, such as Queensland Nuts and Moreton Bay Chestnut. Brazil Nuts are native to South America, while Cashew Nuts are at home in tropical America. In Mediterranean regions, Pine Kernels are eaten like peanuts, either raw or roasted.

Beech
(*Fagus sylvatica*)

Also known as: Common Beech, European Beech

This stately deciduous tree has few equals, often standing 100' (30m) high and forming a canopy of vein-lined, oval and pointed, shiny-green leaves. In early autumn, the tree produces a mass of nuts that, for centuries, have been eaten as food as well as providing forage for pigs, deer, and other animals. Native to woodlands of western and central Europe, including Corsica, Sicily, and Greece, it has been planted in many temperate regions in both hemispheres, from where it has spread into the wild.

You'll find it: In well-drained, open woodland, parks, and grassland, especially where the soil is chalky.

Nuts: Known as beech mast, each nut is triangular, ⅝" (1.5cm) long, and borne in pairs. They are enclosed in a hard, woody, pear-shaped, four-lobed husk and covered in bristles. Beech trees bear nuts only once every three or four years, but when this happens their harvest is prodigious.

Harvesting the nuts: These ripen and fall in early to mid-autumn. Collect as soon as possible, before they are taken by woodland animals, such as squirrels and deer, then place in slatted boxes in a ventilated, gently warm room. Some may need to dry slightly if previously dampened by rain.

Using the nuts: Highly nutritious, the nuts are eaten raw or roasted and salted. Additionally, freshly harvested nuts yield up to 20 percent of their volume in an oil rich in minerals, vitamins, and proteins. Extracting the oil to use as a butter substitute as well as in general cooking involves cleaning the beech mast, removing the husks, and placing in a liquidizer or fine-mincing machine. Put the pulp-like material in a muslin bag and press to extract the oil, then pour resulting oil into dry, sterilized, well-sealed jars. It needs to be used within a few months.

Hazel
(*Corylus avellana*)

Also known as: Cob, Cobnut, European Filbert, European Hazelnut, Filbeard, Filbert, Nutall

The deciduous, shrub-like hazel grows up to 20' (6m) high and you will notice its pendulous, bright-yellow, male catkins in mid- and late winter, long before its clusters of nuts are ready to be harvested in autumn. The female catkins are less apparent, being short and bud-like. Broadly oval, tooth-edged green leaves appear in spring and assume rich yellow shades in autumn.

Native to the British Isles, western Asia, and as far south as the Iberian Peninsula, it also grows in other temperate climates, including regions in North America.

You'll find it: Growing in hedgerows and at shoulder height or less, a result of being regularly cut back; also in woods and on scrubland.

Nuts: Round to oval, each nut is ½"–¾" (1.2–1.8cm) long and borne in clusters of up to four in autumn. Each has a hard brown shell partially enclosed in a thick, deeply lobed green husk.

Harvesting the nuts: They remain on the tree until ripe and fall off in the latter part of early autumn. At this stage, the husks (the protective outer parts) will have changed from green to brown. The nuts inside should be firm; if gathered too early, they will be soft and tasteless and not store well. Remove the husks and store the nuts, still in their shells, in a warm, dry place, but do not allow them to dry out fully. When ripe, the shell naturally falls away from the nut.

Using the nuts: Highly nutritious and eaten raw, the nuts are chopped for adding to salads or used as a substitute for almonds. The ground nuts can be blended with milk or yogurt to make a nutritious smoothie using one-part nuts to three-parts milk (add honey to taste). Hazel nuts are also delicious roasted, and are good added to cereals, breads, and cakes. The pressed nuts also yield a very good oil for salads and cooking.

Common Oak
(*Quercus robur*)

Also known as: English Oak, Pedunculate Oak, Truffle Oak

This lofty, often 80' (25m) high deciduous tree is better known for its timber than its ability to provide food. However, nearly 2,000 years ago, the Roman writer Pliny the Younger (61–112 CE) wrote of 13 varieties of oak tree with acorns that could be ground to produce a bread-making flour. Nearly 1,000 years ago, the English Domesday Book described acorns being fed to hogs.

It is native to most of Europe and the Middle East, and is grown and cultivated abundantly in other temperate regions, such as North America, New Zealand, and the Cape Provinces.

You'll find it: In forests, but not where other trees tightly encroach upon it. You will also see it in open countryside and alongside hedgerows and paths. It grows best in warm temperate regions, as late spring frosts damage early developing shoots.

Acorns: A small, rounded nut (botanically a fruit), the humble acorn is well known. Each acorn usually takes a couple of seasons to mature and is formed of a cup that holds the nut. Trees do not usually produce acorns until 20 years old and may not crop until about 40 years old.

Harvesting the nuts: Trees shed their acorns (when ripe) in early autumn, usually slightly earlier than the fall of leaves. Some acorns will be green but most are brown.

Using the nuts: For thousands of years, preparing flour from acorns has been traditional among native people of many lands; in times of famine, it became an essential food for many people. Today, it is regaining popularity, especially among back-to-nature enthusiasts. In North America, indigenous peoples are said to have mixed clay with acorn flour (at a ratio, by weight, of one-part washed clay to twenty-parts flour). The resulting bread is claimed to be sweet and to rise as if yeast had been added.

Acorn Coffee

In times of hardship, coffee-drinkers have turned to acorns as a coffee substitute. Many other plants, including dandelions, chicory, and grains of corn and rye, are also used to produce a coffee-type drink. Here is one way to create a nutty-tasting acorn coffee:

1. Gather fallen acorns, remove their cupped bases, and place in boiling water until soft. Allow to cool slightly, then remove the shells.
2. Cut them in half or quarters. Put in a microwave on low until dry.
3. Place on a baking tray in a warm oven and roast until brown.
4. Once cool, place in a coffee grinder or kitchen blender, and grind to the consistency of coffee grounds.
5. Use grounds to make drip coffee or espresso as you would with regular coffee grounds.

Acorn Flour

The flour can be used in place of wheat; it is ideal for making pancakes, muffins and, of course, acorn bread.

1. Gather fallen acorns, green or brown, immediately as they are available; do not let them remain on the grass to become dirty and wet.
2. Place in a clean bucket; expect each container to produce half that amount of flour.
3. Arrange the acorns on a baking tray and roast for 20–30 minutes in an oven at 250°F (120°C). This will both dry them and kill any insects lurking inside. When cool, crack off the now-brittle shells to release the acorns.
4. Place the acorns in a muslin bag and immerse in water for two weeks, changing it two or three times each day. This removes most of the tannins, which if left impart a bitter taste to the flour.
5. Either sun-dry on a windowsill or place in a just-warm oven until totally free from moisture. Store the acorns in clean, moisture-proof jars or immediately grind into a flour. If stored, use as soon as possible.

Sweet Chestnut
(*Castanea sativa*)

Also known as: Eurasian Chestnut, European Chestnut, Spanish Chestnut

A large deciduous tree, up to 100' (30m) high, the sweet chestnut produces nuts in mid- to late autumn that can be eaten raw or roasted. Its distinctive, shiny, deep green, narrowly oval leaves are edged in soft spines. Yellow, erect, or spreading male catkins, up to 6" (15cm) long, appear in mid-summer, while the green female flowers (borne at the bases of male catkins) are sparse, but by autumn, will have developed into nuts.

Native to Europe, North Africa, southern Turkey, and western Iran, it has been planted and established in many temperate climates, growing across the Mediterranean region, from the Caspian Sea to the Atlantic Ocean. It is also well known in North America.

You'll find it: Usually in woods surrounded by other trees, or in parks and open countryside. Sometimes it is coppiced (cut down to near ground level in late winter) every 10–15 years to produce young, straight stems used for fencing.

Nuts: Triangular, bright red-brown nuts, borne in twos or threes and each ¾"–1¼" (1.8–3cm) across, are enclosed in pale green husks. These husks, often known as burs, are covered with prickles.

Harvesting the nuts: Trees start to shed their nuts in mid-autumn; you will not be able to reach most of them, but they can be knocked off by using a stick. They can be eaten raw if the husk (which is prickly) and bitter inner skin are removed. But they are more often roasted: Slit the husks and either put them on a grate close to a fire or in hot ash. As a guide to when they are ready, put an uncut one next to them, and when its outer parts burst (usually with a bang), the others are ready to eat.

Using the nuts: Apart from eating the nuts raw or roasted, they can be ground or chopped and used in soup, as stuffing for turkey, in jams, and cakes. Small nuts can be ground into flour for making bread or pancakes. The yellowish, slightly fragrant flour is ideal in cakes and breads but is usually reluctant to rise; therefore, add an equal amount of wheat flour.

Walnut
(*Juglans regia*)

Also known as: English Walnut, Persian Walnut, Madeira Nut

Native to China, west and central Asia, and southeastern Europe, this large, deciduous tree, up to 100' (30m) high, is now widely naturalized in Europe. It has also been planted in other countries, where it has spread. In North America, however, the native Black Walnut (*Juglans nigra*) is more popular and widespread.

The large, distinctive, shiny green leaves of seven to nine leaflets assume rich shades in autumn.

You'll find it: It is a warmth-loving tree; in cool temperate areas, established and earlier cultivated trees in old woodland and parks often produce self-sown seedlings. It also grows in warm, sheltered hedgerows.

Nuts: The outer casing of the nut, about 2" (5cm) across, is known as the hull. Inside it is the shell, which encloses the nut; the nut is the part that is eaten. Walnuts are one of the most popular nuts for eating and baking.

Harvesting the nuts: Usually harvested when ripe in mid-autumn, having changed from green to brown. Wait until the nuts have fallen as many will have split hulls; an indication of ripeness is when the tissue between the hull and the shell turns brown. At this stage, fallen hulls can be gathered from the ground or low branches can be shaken to loosen them.

Using the nuts: Completely remove the hulls, usually by pulling them apart, to leave shells with nuts inside. Discard nuts with cracked shells. Place intact nuts in the sun to dry fully, usually for a couple of weeks. They can then be stored in a cool, dry place for several months.

They are often used as late autumn and winter "treats," chopped in cakes and biscuits. Walnuts are delicious with pears and any blue cheese in a winter salad. Shelled nuts can be kept in the refrigerator for up to five months and in the freezer for more than a year.

In addition to ripe walnuts, you can use young, green fruits, gathered before the nutcase hardens; these are sometimes pickled in vinegar for later use.

Mushrooms, Truffles, and Other Edible Fungi

Throughout the centuries, mushrooms have gained a dark and sinister reputation. Certainly, some fungi are deadly poisonous when eaten, while many others are a valuable source of food and are highly prized by chefs and foragers throughout the world. Identifying fungi that can be eaten is not easy, as apart from their limited growing and harvesting period each year (when you can get to know and identify them), many often change shape and color throughout their lives.

It is vitally important that you correctly identify any fungi you collect and plan to eat. The best way to gain knowledge is by learning from someone who knows fungi well—some experts offer courses and lead guided forays in the autumn. And although most mushrooms are relatively easy to identify, there are a number of poisonous look-alikes, and about 20 species that are very, very dangerous indeed!

Unless you are very familiar with a species, do not rely on the photographs or illustrations in a book for identification, especially since many change their appearance throughout their life cycle. If you are not sure about the identification of a particular specimen you wish to eat and cannot with certainty identify it, discard it. Place it in a plastic bag (so that children and family pets cannot sample it) and put in a trash bin.

If, by chance, you become unwell after eating a fungus, contact a doctor immediately; if possible, take along a sample of the particular fungi. Additionally, write down the name of the species you think you have eaten, as this may lead to rapid identification of the "lookalike" fungi you have mistakenly consumed.

Remember that, although symptoms from some poisonous fungi may arise within minutes, others take several days to emerge.

Foraging, Picking, and Eating Checks

Even if you are confident in your ability to identify fungi, there are still a few things to keep in mind:

- [ ] **Ensure you have legal rights to take the fungi.** Do not walk in private land or destroy growing crops.

- [ ] **Do not forage for fungi on a wet day** as many are highly porous, which spoils their texture and taste.

- [ ] Before picking fungi, **check that it complies with its description and picture**. Remember that color, size, and shape may vary during its growth.

- [ ] **Do not pull fungi directly out of the ground.** Instead, carefully twist its stem until it comes away from the soil.

- [ ] Before placing fungi in a well-ventilated basket, use a sharp knife to **cut off the stem's base**.

- [ ] **Check for maggots or insects** in the cap area; if present in large numbers, throw the fungi away. Also discard fungi that are decaying or reveal white gills (many poisonous types have this characteristic).

- [ ] Before eating, either raw or cooked, **brush off dirt**. If it is necessary to wash fungi, immediately dry the surface with a paper towel.

- [ ] When you get your fungi home, **recheck their authenticity**. Then place in a well-ventilated room and use within 24 hours.

BLEWITS:
Wood Blewit
(*Lepista nuda*)

Also known as: Pied Bleu

A largish mushroom, once listed as *Clitocybe nuda*, with a lilac to purple-pink cap 2½"–5" (6–13cm) across, convex or shield-shaped; with age it assumes reddish shades. The entire mushroom has a sweet and perfume-like scent, with thick, lilac-blue flesh. It is common and widespread across the British Isles, throughout mainland Europe, and in many other parts of the world, including North America.

You'll find it: In coniferous and deciduous woodland, as well as gardens.

Harvesting the fungi: From autumn to early winter.

Eating the fungi: Best cooked rather than eaten fresh. Eat soon after gathering as they are often infested with fly larvae and do not store well.

BLEWITS:
Field Blewit
(*Lepista saeva*)

Also known as: Blue Leg, Pied Violet

Less common than the Wood Blewit (see page 126), it has a smooth, slightly domed cap up to 4½" (12cm) across and 2½" (6cm) high; old ones have flatter caps and sometimes develop wavy edges. The cap is grayish or brown, tinged lilac or purple, while the stem is whitish with blue streaks and slightly bulbous at its base. The whole fungi has a strong, sweet, perfume-like scent with white to gray-pink flesh. It is widespread in the British Isles and most parts of mainland Europe. It is also reported in North America and appears in some field guides.

You'll find it: On grassland and occasionally in lightly shaded woods; it mostly grows in chalky conditions.

Harvesting the fungi: Late summer to very late autumn.

Eating the fungi: They can be eaten fresh (but sometimes cause indigestion) so are usually cooked. Eat soon after gathering as they are often infested with fly larvae and do not store well. Excellent when sautéed in butter or as an addition to omelets.

Cep
(*Boletus edulus*)

Also known as: King Bolete, Penny Bun, Penny Bun Boletus, Porcini

This large wild mushroom is one of the safest to gather as there are virtually no poisonous species that closely resemble it. On maturity, its cap is 3"–10" (7.5–25cm) across, slightly sticky to touch, convex when young but flattening with age. The cap is usually red-brown, fading to white near the edges, with the whole top darkening as it matures. The stem is stout and swollen, pale brown, and revealing a network of raised, white veins toward its top. The flesh, which has a mild nutty flavor, is firm and white when young, becoming spongy with age.

Ceps occur abundantly in the Northern Hemisphere, across Asia, Europe, and North America. Additionally, it has been introduced into Australia, New Zealand, southern Africa, and Brazil.

You'll find it: In coniferous and deciduous woodland and especially in grassy clearings. It is common in beech woods.

Harvesting the fungi: Late summer to mid-autumn and sometimes slightly later.

Eating the fungi: It is low in fat and digestible carbohydrates, but high in vitamins, proteins, and minerals. Ceps are superb when sliced and eaten fresh, although widely eaten sautéed. They are frequently dried and used in casseroles, soups, and risottos. It is also good in pasta dishes as well as lending itself to being stuffed with chopped onions, bacon, parsley, and breadcrumbs, then baked until tender.

Other Edible Boletus

Bay Boletus (*Boletus badius*): Chestnut-brown cap, 2"–5" (5–13cm) wide, with fairly soft, white or lemon-yellow flesh. It is ready for harvesting from late summer to mid- or even late autumn. It occurs in both coniferous and deciduous woodland, especially under beech trees.

Yellow-Cracked Boletus (*Boletus subtomentosus*): Olive-yellow to rich yellow cap, 2"–4½" (5–12cm) wide, becoming red-brown with age. The flesh is white or pale lemon yellow. Usually ready for harvesting from late summer and into early autumn. Again, it is often seen in deciduous woodland.

Chanterelle
(*Cantharellus cibarius*)

Also known as: Chanterelle Commune, Girolles, Golden Chanterelle

The funnel-shaped cap is egg-yellow to orange-yellow, sometimes paler, with flesh that has an apricot scent but when eaten produces a fruity and mildly peppery taste. It is up to 4" (10cm) wide, sometimes slightly more, initially round and flat, but later with a depressed center and assuming its distinctive funnel shape with irregularly waved edges. However, there are a number of other mushrooms that look similar, so make sure that you are absolutely correct in your identification.

It is found in Europe, from Scandinavia to the Mediterranean Sea, as well as in North America.

You'll find it: In woodland, especially under oaks, birches, beech, and pine trees, and where the soil is slightly acid.

Harvesting the fungi: Gather from mid-summer through to early autumn, depending on the rain fall and temperature.

Eating the fungi: After cutting, trim the base and use a soft brush to clean the flesh. Chanterelles are inevitably used fresh since they do not dry well. There are many ways to eat them, including sautéed in butter with parsley and used as a side dish. Chanterelles are also delicious when added to scrambled eggs, omelets, and pasta dishes. Pan-roasted chanterelles make a great accompaniment to lemon sole and oysters.

Poisonous Mushrooms to Avoid

There are several "lookalike" species that must be avoided, including:

False Chanterelle (*Hygrophoropsis aurantiaca*), which is inedible.

Jack O'Lantern (*Omphalotus olearius*) also known as Copper Trumpet, which is extremely poisonous.

Deadly Webcap (*Cortinarius rubellus*), which is deadly poisonous and causes kidney failure. It was earlier known as *Cortinarius speciosissimus*.

Poisonous Mushrooms to Avoid

There are several "lookalike" species that occur in similar situations and close to Fairy Ring Champignon that must be avoided, including:

Ivory Clitocybe (*Clitocybe dealbata*), which is deadly poisonous.

False Champignon (*Clitocybe rivulosa*), which is also deadly poisonous.

Fairy Ring Champignon
(*Marasmius oreades*)

Also known as: Fairy Ring Mushroom, Scotch Bonnet

This mushroom species grows in fairy rings on lawns; this one—as well as a few others—is edible, but others are not, so take great care with identification. It develops brownish caps, often tinged pink to pale red-brown, up to 2" (5cm) across, initially domed then flattened and with even, uplifted edges. This mushroom has a creamy, woody (often claimed to resemble sawdust), mushroom-like scent.

This mushroom is native and widespread in Europe and North America, especially in the east.

You'll find it: In lawns, pastures, fields with short grass, and along roadsides. It forms circles of fungi, disfiguring lawns, and golf courses.

Harvesting the fungi: Late spring to late autumn, but most abundant in summer.

Eating the fungi: The white-to-buff flesh tends to be thin and rather tough, but with a pleasant, mushroom-like flavor. Caps have the tendency to dry quickly when they become hard and leathery and change to a pale tan color. Stems are usually discarded if they become dry.

Traditionally, the caps have been threaded on to strings (with a button on the bottom) and hung up to dry, where they can remain in a warm but well-ventilated room for several weeks. They can be reconstituted by soaking in clean water for several hours. Alternatively, instead of rehydrating in water, simply drop them as they are into soups and stews.

Field Mushroom
(*Agaricus campestris*)

Also known as: Champignons, Common Field Mushroom, Common Mushroom, Hot-bed Mushroom, Meadow Mushroom, Pink Bottoms, Rosé des prés

An attractive mushroom with creamy white caps, about 1¾"–4" (3–10cm) wide, on stems ⅞"–2½" (2–6cm) long. Initially, caps are dome shaped, later flattening slightly and, with age, assume a brownish tinge. The white flesh is slightly red-pink to brown when cut. It is closely related to the cultivated Button Mushroom (*Agaricus bisporus*), which is widely sold in shops and supermarkets. The field mushroom is widespread in temperate areas of Europe, Asia, northern Africa, New Zealand, Australia, and North America.

You'll find it: In large fairy rings on lawns, in meadows and fields, especially where manured by livestock.

Harvesting the fungi: From mid-summer to late autumn; especially abundant where the climate is mild and after showers of rain.

Eating the fungi: At their best when sliced and fresh in salads, although some claim that the flavor intensifies when cooked, especially with large and mature specimens. Its uses are endless—try in soups and risottos, make mushroom pâté, or sauté in butter and serve on toast covered with their own juices.

Poisonous Mushrooms to Avoid

There are several "lookalike" species that must be avoided:

Destroying Angel (*Amanita virosa*): Take care when picking field mushrooms at the button stage as it then resembles this infamous mushroom. This fatal fungus has the sickly sweet scent of honey and a pure white cap that is frequently slightly sticky to the touch.

Destroying Angel

Death Cap (*Amanita phalloides*) is another deadly fungus sometimes confused with the field mushroom.

Death Cap

Deadly Fibrecap (*Inocybe patouillardii*) occurs in similar locations as field mushroom but is deadly poisonous.

Deadly Fibrecap

Giant Puffball
(*Calvatia gigantea*)

Sometimes known as *Langermannia gigantea*, this is a monster of the fungus world; giant specimens are said to have been mistaken for sheep! Usually it is 8"–20" (20–50cm) across. The flesh is white and firm when young and this is when it should be eaten; later it becomes yellowish, then brown (when it is best left alone). Its matte surface is white at first and finely textured like kid gloves. Later, the surface discolors to pale olive-brown.

It is widespread and common in Britain, mainland Europe and North America, as well as temperate areas throughout the world. In some countries in Europe, such as parts of Poland, it is now protected; in others, including Lithuania and Norway, it is considered rare. In many other countries, there is concern about its decreasing numbers, therefore, do not over-forage this fungus.

You'll find it: In fields, gardens, and deciduous forests, along hedgerows and edges of fields, and on banks. It is sometimes found growing among stinging nettles, which offers it some protection from animals and foragers.

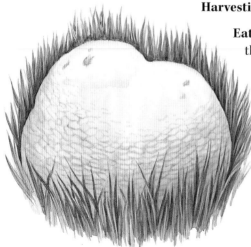

Harvesting the fungi: In late summer into autumn.

Eating the fungi: It should be eaten while young when the flesh is firm and white. Try it thinly sliced and added in salads. Alternatively, thicker slices can be coated in beaten egg and breadcrumbs, then sautéed like cutlets—serve with a squeeze of lemon. You can also add it cubed to stews and casseroles, where it takes on a delicious meaty texture.

Another Edible Puffball

The **Mosaic Puffball** (*Calvatia utriformis*) has a white to cream, pear-shaped body that can reach 10" (25cm) across and 8" (20cm) high with white flesh that, with age, becomes green-yellow and later dark olive-brown. Its outer surface cracks into hexagonal patches as it ages, hence its common name.

It is widespread in northern temperate regions and found on pastures and sandy heaths during late summer and into autumn; the flesh is edible when young.

Morel
(*Morchella esculenta*)

Also known as: Common Morel, Dryland Fish, Haystack, May Mushroom, Morel Mushroom, Molly Moocher, Morille Comestible, Sponge Morel, True Morel, Yellow Morel

This distinctive fungus, growing 4"–6" (10–20cm) high, has a cap that begins life as a tightly compressed grayish sponge with lighter-colored ridges. It then expands to create a large, yellowish, honeycomb-like sponge with ridges and deep pits. The stout, sometimes twisted, white stem becomes yellowish and reddish with age while the cap is hollow.

It is widely found in North America, especially in eastern North America and the Midwest. Additionally, it is found in Canada, Bulgaria, Brazil, the British Isles, and throughout other parts of Europe and Asia. It is also known to be present in Australia, but is rare.

You'll find it: Usually in woodland clearings, especially in chalky soil around deciduous trees, old orchards, bases of well-established hedgerows, and where vegetation has been cleared through burning. It grows singly or in groups.

Harvesting the fungi: Mid- to late spring—it has a narrow time band when it can be gathered each year. However, in northern parts of North America, gathering is usually delayed until early summer, when the temperature rises and the weather improves. This delay also applies to colder regions in Europe.

Eating the fungi: Morels should not be eaten raw as they contain small amounts of toxins that are removed through cooking. Because of their honeycomb-like hollow structure, morels become a refuge for insects. Cut lengthways and wash in running water (take care to dry in a warm room) or dust with a small, soft artist's brush. Morels are popular in soups and stews, and are excellent stuffed. They can also be sautéed in butter.

Poisonous Mushrooms to Avoid

There are "lookalike" species that must be avoided, including **False Morel** or Turban Fungus (*Gyromitra esculenta*). It may be fatal when eaten raw and very harmful to some even when cooked.

Oyster Mushroom
(*Pleurotus ostreatus*)

Also known as: Flat Mushroom, Oyster Cap, Oyster Fungus

Sometimes considered to be flavorless, this bracket fungus was widely collected during times of food scarcity, especially as it is easy to gather, grows in colonies, and dries and keeps well. The caps, 2"–6" (5–15cm) across but occasionally slightly larger, do not usually have stems and grow directly from their host. The caps are deep blue-gray to gray-brown, depending on their age; the narrow, crowded gills are white to grayish.

The entire fungus has a pleasant, almond-like scent. It is widespread in many temperate and subtropical regions throughout the world, including North America, the British Isles, Europe, and Asia.

You'll find it: Because it is a primary decomposer of dead and dying trunks and branches, you will find it among deciduous trees, especially beech and ash. It is only occasionally found on conifers. However, it does not like growing near stinging nettles, which like an acidic soil.

Harvesting the fungi: Throughout the year, especially in warm and moist areas. In temperate regions, they are mainly gathered in autumn and winter. It should be harvested while young, since the flesh becomes tough and the flavor unpleasant with age.

Eating the fungi: It is considered a delicacy in Asian cuisine and frequently served on its own or in soups, stews, casseroles, stuffed, or in stir-fry recipes. Try it lightly grilled. It can also be dried successfully and stores well in jars under good olive oil or wine vinegar.

Shaggy Parasol
(*Chlorophyllum rhacodes*)

Formerly known as *Lepiota rhacodes* and *Macrolepiota rhacodes*, this mushroom has a distinctive cap that is 3"–7" (7.5–18cm) across when mature. When young, however, it is smaller and resembles a drumstick. It can be both dull- or dirty-brown and has a rough, scaly, and shaggy appearance (hence the name). On maturity, the cap flattens. The soft white flesh becomes red-brown if cut or bruised, with a strong, pleasant smell. The stem, up to 6" (15cm) high, is whitish and bulbous-based.

Note that there are a number of poisonous species that resemble these fungi, so be especially careful about identification. The form *hortensis* is sometimes found in manure-rich gardens and large old greenhouses. It is more robust and larger than the species and reveals an almost white, coarse, scaly cap, brown at its center, with an extremely bulbous stem.

The species is fairly widespread in North America, but usually seen from the Rocky Mountains eastwards, although also known in California. It is also seen in the British Isles and throughout Europe.

You'll find it: In woodland and especially where there is a deep litter of leaves or needles from conifers. It flourishes in rich soil in light shade.

Harvesting the fungi: Mid-summer through to late autumn.

Eating the fungi: Although it is a good edible mushroom, some people react unfavorably to it, so take care when eating for the first time. To be on the safe side, it should always be cooked. Also discard the stems of all but the very youngest of specimens. It can be added to soups, casseroles, and stews, as well as being sautéed. It also makes a welcome accompaniment to bacon in a bacon and mushroom quiche. These fungi can be dried and then reconstituted.

Poisonous Mushrooms to Avoid

There are "lookalike" species that must be avoided, including **False Parasol** or Green-Spored Parasol (*Chlorophyllum molybdites*). It is a widespread, highly poisonous lookalike species (it is apparently the most commonly consumed poisonous mushroom in North America). It also grows in similar habitat to the edible shaggy parasol and parasol mushrooms.

Truffle
(*Tuber aestivum*)

Also known as: Summer Truffle

The truffle is perhaps one of the best-known and highly prized edible fungi, widely sought by chefs and very expensive to buy. It grows and develops underground in association with beech, sweet chestnut, and evergreen oak trees, and is usually seen when 2"–6" (5–15cm) across. Irregularly round, dark brown, lumpy, and warty, it has firm white flesh that turns buff with a network of white veins.

It has a wide distribution and is found across Europe, from Spain to Eastern Europe and from Sweden to northern Africa. Prior to the 20th century, it was widely seen in Britain, but is now becoming rare. It is also found in North America, Central and South America, the Middle East, and Asia.

You'll find it: Grows underground in broad-leaved woods on chalky soil; it is especially found in Beech woods.

Harvesting the fungi: From late summer to autumn. The traditional way to find truffles is to use dogs or female pigs trained to detect their scent, which is strong, sweet, and pleasant. Without the use of dogs or pigs they are almost undetectable, and the only chance of finding them is to know where they have been found before. Keep in mind that truffles are a rare species, so observe the foraging code.

Eating the fungi: Wash and remove all traces of soil from the surface of the truffle and don't peel. Pat dry with a paper towel. Use as soon as possible after harvesting or preserve in olive oil—this has the added benefit of creating truffle-flavored oil. Only the thinnest sliver of truffle is required to impart an incredible flavor.

Eating Truffles

- Wash and remove all traces of soil from the outside of truffles as they are used without being peeled. Use a paper towel to dry them thoroughly.
- Use as soon as possible after being harvested.
- The fungus is grated or scraped on food and into sauces and soups, just before being eaten.
- Chefs recommend that veal, chicken, fish, soufflés, pasta, rice, and omelets benefit from the addition of truffles.

Seaweeds

Seaweeds are rich in proteins and vitamins, and in many places, are still collected and eaten to supplement diets, especially during times of food scarcity. These plants were an important part of the diet when modern man emerged from Africa about 80,000 years ago and beach-combed his way around many parts of the world.

Unlike most land plants that reproduce through flowers and seeds, seaweed perpetuates itself through spores that develop into plants, which in turn secure themselves to mud, sand, rocks, or stones by means of "holdfasts." These vary in size and form: those that secure stem-bases in muddy conditions often have large, spreading, root-like natures, while those found in sandy soil are bulb-like and flexible. Those that secure stems to smooth surfaces, such as rocks and stones, have holdfasts that literally glue them into position. None of these methods enable stems to extract food from their support. If they did, foundation materials, such as mud or sand, would eventually be eroded and fail to give support. Instead, seaweeds derive their nutrients from chemicals in the water.

When harvesting seaweeds, be careful not to rip off all the fronds and leave little of the plant remaining; these species need as much consideration for rejuvenation as land plants. Freely floating pieces of seaweed can be gathered without causing damage, but if you decide to cut pieces from growing plants, do not do this close to the "holdfast."

Always wash fronds thoroughly before eating, since the water may be polluted with emissions piped into coastal waters. Also check that no small marine creatures remain attached to your foraged pieces of seaweed before taking it home with you. If there are, carefully remove them and put them safely back into the water.

Bladder Wrack
(*Fucus vesiculosus*)

Also known as: Black Tang, Black Tany, Bladder Fucus, Sea Oak, Popweed, Rock Wrack, and Rock Weed

A widespread and common seaweed with branching fronds bearing conspicuous bladders that are variable in size and shape. Apart from being edible, it has been used as food for livestock and a fertilizer for soil improvement on account of its high nutrient content.

Bladder wrack is found on the shores of the North Sea, the western Baltic Sea, and the Atlantic and Pacific Oceans, as well as the shores of the British Isles, Atlantic shores of Europe, Northern Russia, Greenland, Canary Islands, Morocco, and North America.

You'll find it: Along North Atlantic shores in estuaries and the middle and lower shorelines attached to rocks, timberwork, and other structures. Also, in sheltered areas, between high and low tides, and below intertidal areas where undercurrents are slight.

Fronds: The dark olive-brown, flattened branching fronds, up to 6' (1.8m) long, have prominent mid-ribs with spherical air bladders peppered along them.

Harvesting the fronds: Harvest the tender young lateral branches in summer and wash thoroughly.

Using the fronds: These can be chopped and dried and added to soups, or used fresh as a thickening agent in fish, meat, and vegetable dishes. It is a particularly rich source of iodine.

Knotted Wrack

(*Ascophyllum nodosum*), also known as Egg Wrack, Knotted Kelp, and Norwegian Kelp, is another useful seaweed to the forager. It is found in many of the same regions as bladder wrack. Its fronds are olive-green, can reach 6' (1.8m) long, and are attached to rocks. They do not have long stems and bear large, egg- shaped air bladders—some as large as walnuts— at regular intervals along the fronds. Cut the fronds in summer and wash under running water. It is widely used as an emulsifier in ice cream and soft drinks, in confectionery, jellies, puddings, and as a thickener for soups.

Carrageen
(*Chondrus crispus*)

Also known as: Carrageen Moss, Irish Moss, Jelly Moss, Pearl Moss

In addition to its food value, carrageen is used as a medical tonic and a stabilizer in milk products, including ice cream. It is also ideal as a thickener in soups and as a basis for edible sausage skins. It grows along the rocky parts of the Atlantic coast of Europe and North America. It is common around the shores of Ireland and Iceland, the Faroe Islands, and ranges from the western Baltic Sea to southern Spain. It can also be found on the Atlantic coasts of Canada, and from California to Japan.

You'll find it: In intertidal regions and shallow areas below low tide. It is usually attached to rocks by a stem that varies in length.

Fronds: Soft but firm and flexible and varying from greenish yellow, through red to dark purple or purple-brown. The color usually bleaches in strong sunlight. Fronds are up to 8" (20cm) long, with repeated branching that creates an impression of a fan.

Harvesting the fronds: Best during mid- to late spring by removing young parts.

Using the fronds: They are very versatile and can be used fresh or dried. Wash the fronds thoroughly in running water shortly after gathering. To dry the fronds, wash then spread out on a clean surface out of doors and protect from wind-borne dirt. Repeat washing or leave in the rain. When dry, cut off tough parts and store young pieces in clean jars.

Blancmange and Jelly

- **Blancmange:** To make, use one measure of seaweed to three measures of milk, then simmer until the fronds dissolve. Sugar and flavorings can be added to suit your tastes.
- **Jelly:** To make, use the same measures as the blancmange but replace the milk with water (or a mixture of water and fruit juice). Again, add flavorings and colorings.
- For both jellies and blancmanges, sieve the mixture, pour into a jelly mold, and allow to set. You can introduce flavors, such as ginger, vanilla, cinnamon, brandy, or whisky for variety.

Dulse
(*Palmaria palmata*)

Also known as: Dillisk, Dilsk, Red Dulse, Sea Lettuce; Creathnach

Native to the shores of the North Atlantic and Baltic Sea, dulse is a common seaweed that has been gathered as a foodstuff for centuries. It may be divided into several strap-like segments, or it may appear as a single blade, and it is also variable in size and color with red to brown-red and purple tones. Dulse grows on the northern coasts of the Atlantic and Pacific Oceans, as well as ranging from Portugal to the Baltic Coasts, and the shores of Arctic Russia, Arctic Canada, Alaska, Japan, and North and South Korea.

You'll find it: Attached to rocks along the middle and lower shores and extends below the lowest spring tide mark.

Fronds: The fan-like fronds, up to 12" (30cm) long and usually with five lobes, are tough and dark red. Sometimes, small leaflets appear at the edges of fronds with single, broad, or narrow blades or strap-like segment.

Harvesting the fronds: Harvest from late spring to mid-autumn, collecting the younger, more tender fronds. Don't rip the seaweed up from its base; leave some of the fronds behind. Wash several times in clean water.

Using the fronds: Rich in vitamins, minerals, and trace elements, it has a high protein content. Dulse can be eaten raw or cooked in salads, stir-fries, soups, and casseroles. Dulse has been mixed with mashed potato to make a kind of champ. The leaves were sometimes chewed as a substitute gum. It can also be dried quite successfully, then ground and used as a flavoring.

Dulse Champ

Add Dulse to creamy mashed potatoes to make a version of that great Irish staple, "champ."

INGREDIENTS
- Good handful of dulse
- Small pan of milk
- Mashed potatoes, cooked
- 2 tablespoons butter
- Seasonings, to taste
- Scallions, chopped, to taste

INSTRUCTIONS
1. A couple of hours before serving, wash dulse in running water.
2. Simmer the dulse in milk until tender, about 2 hours.
3. Beat the cooked dulse into hot mashed potatoes with butter, and season to your own taste. Garnish with scallions.

Laver
(*Porphyra umbilicalis*)

Also known as: Purple Laver, Red Seaweed, Stoke

Popular as a food plant, especially as a breakfast delicacy, this seaweed has a long tradition of filling stomachs. It is highly nutritious; rich in protein; carbohydrates; vitamins B, B2, A, and C; plus trace elements and minerals, including iodine. It is popular with vegetarians and widely sold in health shops.

Laver can be found on the temperate gulf of Maine and southern New England, from northern Portugal up to the Faroe Islands, and on the the coasts of the United Kingdom and Ireland.

You'll find it: Abundant on rocks and stones, especially in intertidal areas; it is highly adaptable and able to survive long periods of exposure to the air as well as being battered by wave action.

Fronds: The broad, membranous, translucent wavy-edged, irregularly shaped fronds, up to 8" (20cm) long, are initially green but soon become purple-red, with a thin but strong, polythene-like texture.

Harvesting the fronds: Cut during spring and summer, and wash in clean water several times.

Using the fronds: Fresh fronds make an excellent wrapper when baking fish. To cook, repeat the washing, then boil in only a small amount of water until soft and with the appearance of a very dark, spinach-like purée. This purée is then coated in oatmeal, fried, and eaten with bacon and eggs, although small boiled potatoes and butter are another choice. It also goes well in sandwiches and chopped in salads. The purée can also be stored in sterilized jars, which can then be stored in the refrigerator for a short time.

Laverbread

The Welsh make this seaweed into laverbread by boiling the seaweed for several hours, then puréeing and drying the results. It is sold either as it is, or rolled in oatmeal then eaten with bacon, which is considered to be a great treat. It also accompanies lamb, crab, monkfish, and cockles extremely well and can also be made into soup.

Oarweed
(*Laminaria digitata*)

Also known as: Common Kelp, Fingered Tangle, Horsetail Kelp, Kelp, Sea Tangle, Tangle, Kombu

A widespread seaweed that has been used as a source of human food as well as to feed livestock in times of hardship, oarweed is found in the northern Atlantic Ocean, from Greenland south to Cape Cod and in the northeast Atlantic from northern Russia and Iceland south to France. It is most common around the coasts of the British Isles.

You'll find it: Close to the low-water line, where it is regularly covered by water. It also grows well in shallow pools and can soon colonize large areas, anchoring itself to rocks and pebbles with a claw-like holdfast.

Fronds: Brown, usually about 5' (1.5m) long and with finger-like branches. Occasionally, when in large and undisturbed colonies, it is claimed to grow 10' (3m) or more long.

Harvesting the fronds: Cut during spring and early summer to use fresh. Alternatively, they can be harvested and dried in the open in an area sheltered from wind-blown dust. When dry, place in clean jars and put in the refrigerator.

Eating the fronds: Young stems can be eaten fresh (first wash in running water) and are said to resemble the flavor of peanuts. Additionally, they can be made into flour, as well as being added to dishes that contain lentils, vegetables, and rice. Alternatively, they can be washed, shredded, and pickled as a condiment.

Bean Softener

Along with other kelps, oarweed is a traditional constituent of bean-based stews in Japan. It is supposed to speed up the cooking time by softening the beans and adding thickness to the stew. When using kelp in this way, put a few strips of dried kelp in the base of a pan, add the beans, and simmer gently until they are tender.

Gutweed
(*Enteromorpha intestinalis*)

Sometimes known as: Grass Kelp, Sea Grass, Hollow Green Seaweed

Widespread throughout the world, gutweed is also botanically known as *Ulva intestinalis* and looks amazingly like ropes of intestines. It is found in the Bering Sea near Alaska, Puget Sound, across Europe and Asia, and the Baltic and Mediterranean Sea, as well as the shores of the Pacific Ocean.

You will find it: One of the most adaptable seaweeds, flourishing in rocky pools, and brackish water where there is fresh water running through it, as well as on rocks, mud, and sand.

Fronds: The green, unbranched, tubular, inflated fronds are up to 12" (30cm) long. It is an annual and sometimes pieces become detached and float to the surface, where they survive in a floating mass. By the end of summer, the fronds become bleached by the sun.

Harvesting and using the fronds: Gather it in spring or early summer when it is best stir-fried until crisp.

Sea Lettuce
(*Ulva lactuca*)

A cosmopolitan seaweed, it is found on the shores of Europe, west and east coasts of North America, Central America, South America, Caribbean islands, Indian Ocean islands, southwest Asia, Pacific islands, Australia, and New Zealand.

You will find it: Attached to rocks, either between the tidal area or slightly below.

Fronds: Tough, crumple-edged green to dark green, nearly translucent fronds 7" (18cm) long and 12" (30cm) across.

Gathering the fronds: The leaves are much prized and gathered in early spring or summer.

Eating the fronds: Wash thoroughly, chop up, and serve raw in salads. They are also added to soups and are a central part of some Japanese dishes. They also make a great wrap for baked fish.

Shellfish

Shellfish, like seaweeds, have been gathered by humans from beaches and rocks for thousands and thousands of years. Early people would not have realized the benefits of a seafood-rich diet and just considered them to be "stomach fillers," but for us, the benefits are clear. Shellfish are high in protein but low in saturated fats, so help reduce the risk of heart disease, decrease blood pressure, and lower blood fats.

They offer an exciting change in diet for the coastal forager, although care needs to be taken to ensure that all shellfish is clear of contamination from emissions discharged into the sea. Always wash any shellfish thoroughly before eating and ensure they are still alive. Dead shellfish are extremely dangerous to eat and may result in a very unpleasant illness or perhaps a hospital visit.

Killing shellfish humanely presents welfare problems. Dropping them live into saucepans of boiling water is cruel, and although it is the traditional way to kill them, it need not be the method of choice today. Lobsters, crayfish, and crabs once killed by plunging into boiling water are now dispatched more humanely by stunning them electrically. It is fast and efficient, reduces harmful bacteria, and improves their texture and taste. In a fraction of a second, the electrical charge knocks them unconscious, and by sustaining the current, quickly destroys their entire nervous system. Compare this to the three minutes or more it takes for a lobster to die when in it is immersed in boiling water!

These electrical stunners are readily available, and their use is recommended by many animal welfare organizations. The shellfish described in this chapter are much smaller than lobsters, crabs, and crayfish. Unfortunately, at present, there is no electrical stunner available that will kill them; therefore, after cleaning them, place in a freezer prior to dropping in boiling water—this puts them into a dormant state, which alleviates some welfare concerns.

Clam
(*Mya arenaria*)

Also known as: Long-necked Clam, Long Necks, Nannynose, Piss Clams, Sand Gaper, Soft Clam, Soft-shelled Clam, Soft Shells, Steamers

A popular seashore delicacy, a clam has a hinged oval, soft white to pale-gray or brownish shell up to 5" (13cm) across. It buries itself 6"–10" (15–25cm) deep in mud, and extends two long, fused siphons to the surface of the mud to draw in seawater that is filtered for food and then expelled.

Clams are found along the western Atlantic Ocean, from Canada to the southern United States, as well as the United Kingdom in the eastern Atlantic Ocean.

You'll find them: Usually on the middle and lower shorelines, in brackish water and along estuaries. They prefer a sandy-mud base with some gravel.

Harvesting the clams: If pressure is applied to the surface of the area where clams are thought to be, they often eject water from their siphon tips. Dig them up carefully and place in a deep bucket of seawater for a few days so that they clean themselves.

End their lives humanely (see page 157) before scalding in boiling water for 15 minutes. Trim off the siphons.

Eating the clams: Can be steamed whole in their shells, or the flesh removed and fried, baked or boiled, and served with a sauce. They are delicious with pasta—spaghetti alle vongole is a great Italian favorite.

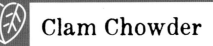

Clam Chowder

INGREDIENTS

- 16–20 clams
- 3–4 bacon slices
- Onion, chopped
- 4 medium potatoes
- 1¾ cups (420ml) milk
- Bay leaf
- Good pinch of salt and pepper
- Parsley, chopped, to taste

INSTRUCTIONS

1. Scrub clams and place in a pan with a bit of water. Cover and cook until the clams open. Discard any that don't open. Take off the heat. Reserve the juice.
2. Fry bacon with onion until cooked.
3. Cube potatoes and place in a separate pot with milk, bay leaf, salt, and pepper. Cook until just tender.
4. Add the bacon and onions, the clams taken from their shells, and reserved clam juice to the pan. Heat through for five minutes.
5. Check the seasoning. Crush some of the potatoes with a fork and garnish with parsley.

Cockle
(*Cerastoderma edule*)

Also known as: Common Cockle

A popular seafood with a ribbed shell up to 2½" (6cm) wide and variable in color, whether cream, light-yellow, or pale brown. Cockles are found around the eastern coastlines of the North Atlantic Ocean, from west Africa to Norway, and along North Sea coasts.

You'll find them: Most abundant on tidal flats, in bays and estuaries, and usually in sandy mud, sand, or fine gravel.

Harvesting the cockles: They are found most often after the tide has gone out and usually in clusters. They are up to 3" (7.5cm) below the surface, so use your hands to reveal them. Do not gather small ones—anything under 1" (2.5cm) wide. Wash off any mud and sand, and carefully place them in a bucket of seawater; leave alone for a day or so until they clean themselves, then put in a bucket of fresh clean water for a few hours to remove the taste of salt.

Eating the cockles: To end their lives, use the most humane method available (see page 157) before scalding them in boiling water. First, however, check that they are alive by prizing open the shell. With their shells open, cockles cook in boiling water within five minutes. They are eaten in many ways, from cooking with bacon, to being made into soups or pies. Cockles are often eaten simply steamed with a shallot vinegar for added zip. Like other forms of seafood, they lend themselves to pasta and rice dishes including risottos, paellas, and also as an ingredient in fish soups and stews.

Common Limpet
(*Patella vulgata*)

Also known as: European Limpet

A well-known seafood with a conical, gray-white shell up to 2½" (6cm) across; those on the lower shoreline have lower shells than ones higher up. Limpets move by means of a muscular "foot," which is yellow, orange, or brown with a green or grayish tint. They graze on algae and seek a resting place when the tide retreats.

This limpet is widely seen on coastlines along the North Atlantic, from the Arctic Circle to Portugal in the south. It has been foraged for centuries as a welcome source of protein.

You'll find them: Attached to rocks and stones from the high- to low-water levels and underwater.

Harvesting the limpets: Choose large specimens from rocks that are washed daily by tides and use a strong knife to prize them from their holding positions. Wash and place in a bucket of seawater for a day or so. Then, put in clean water for a few hours to remove the taste of salt.

To end their lives, use the most humane method available (see page 157) before dropping into boiling water for five or so minutes.

Eating the limpets: Limpet soup is popular, as well as "dressing" large ones and frying them in a little butter, pepper, and vinegar. Small limpets are best boiled.

Common Mussel
(*Mytilus edulis*)

Also known as: Bay Mussel, Blue Mussel, Edible Mussel

Perhaps one of the best-known edible shellfish, common mussels grow up to 4" (10cm) long, with purple, blue, or occasionally brown and bright green smooth shells showing concentric growth lines.

Common mussels are found in coastal areas of the northern Atlantic Ocean, including North America, Europe, and the northern Palearctic; also in the White Sea in Russia to southern France, throughout the British Isles, southwest England, north Wales, and west Scotland.

You'll find them: Between areas of high and low tide, attached to rocks and other hard marine surfaces. They secure themselves in position by thread-like structures that grow from the foot of the mussel.

Harvesting the mussels: Gather and put in a bucket of clean water overnight, then change the water and leave for a further day to remove the salt.

To avoid food poisoning, pick only those from clean, shingle or stony beaches, away from effluent outflows. Before cooking, check that the mussel is alive; discard any with cracked or gapping shells. Never eat dead mussels; those suitable for eating have tightly closed shells or ones that snap shut when tapped.

Eating the mussels: Can be steamed, baked, or fried, taking care not to overcook as they then become tough. Popular in pasta dishes, seafood soups, fish stews, such as bouillabaisse, and Spanish dishes, such as paella.

Mussels in a Parcel

INGREDIENTS

- 2¼ lbs. (1kg) mussels
- 2 garlic cloves
- Handful of parsley
- Small chili pepper
- Olive oil, to taste
- Lemon juice, to taste
- Black pepper, to taste

INSTRUCTIONS

1. Clean and prepare mussels. Preheat oven to 425°F (220°C).
2. Finely chop garlic, parsley, and chili pepper.
3. To make parcels, tear off two large pieces of greaseproof paper and pile the mussels (divided into two) onto the paper.
4. Sprinkle parsley, garlic, and chili over the piles. Drizzle over a little olive oil, a squeeze of lemon, season with black pepper, and tie the parcels.
5. Place on a baking sheet and bake in oven for 5–8 minutes, then serve.

Common Winkle
(*Littorina littorea*)

Also known as: Common Periwinkle, Edible Periwinkle, Winkle

This small, edible shellfish is usually about ½" (1cm) high at maturity but occasionally 1¼" (3cm). It has a dark gray or black conical shell that becomes smooth with age.

It is native to coastal areas of the northeastern North Atlantic, from northern Spain to Scandinavia and Russia. It can be found in the northeastern and northwestern Atlantic Ocean, including northern Spain, France, the British Isles, Scandinavia, Russia, and Nigeria.

You'll find them: Native to a large area, from the upper shoreline down to the water's edge; also, on mudflats and in estuaries.

Harvesting the winkles: Place them in a bucket of clean water overnight to free them from sand and grit.

Eating the winkles: End their lives using the most humane method available (see page 157). They are cooked by gently simmering for about ten minutes. Their meat is high in protein but low in fat, and needs "winkling" out of their shells with a pin. Like cockles, they were and are traditionally sold from seafood stalls in pint jugs accompanied by a sharp vinegar dressing and eaten on the street.

Eating Winkles

Winkles used to be an essential part of the diet in countries where these useful little creatures were harvested. Nowadays, there are few recipes for winkles, although they have been cooked in omelets, used in fishy stews, and served with mustard, lemon, and garlic. You might try your foraged and steamed winkles dipped in a garlicy mayonnaise, or make them into a sandwich with some watercress, a good grinding of pepper, and a squeeze of lemon.

Oyster
(*Ostrea edulis*)

Also known as: Colchester Native Oyster, European Flat Oyster, Mud Oyster

Nowadays, oysters are difficult to find because they have been excessively harvested in earlier years. However, they are worth seeking out. There are numerous kinds of oyster but generally are oval- or pear-shaped, with a rough and scaly surface, off-white, yellowish, or cream in color with light brown or bluish concentric bands. Sizes vary, usually to 4" (10cm) long.

Oyster is native to western European coastlines, from Morocco in the south to Spitsbergen in Norway. They are found in Europe (the British Isles, France, Norway, Morocco, much of the British Isles, and the Mediterranean coast), as well as eastern North America from Maine to Rhode Island, and have been an important addition to human diets for millennia. These days, oysters are intensively farmed and the market for them is prodigious.

You'll find them: In shallow coastal water with firm mud, rocks, muddy sand, or gravel bases.

Harvesting and eating the oysters: Usually eaten raw, with lemon and Tabasco sauce. Be alert to contamination as a result of pollution.

Grilled Oysters

INGREDIENTS

- 12 oysters
- 2 tablespoons butter
- ½ teaspoon garlic, chopped
- ½ teaspoon parsley, chopped
- 3 tablespoons breadcrumbs, toasted
- Salt and pepper, to taste

INSTRUCTIONS

1. Steam open oysters in a large pot; replace oysters on the flattened half of the shell.
2. Mash together butter, garlic, parsley, and breadcrumbs to make herby butter.
3. Dot each oyster with a bit of the herby butter.
4. Season with salt and pepper.
5. Half-fill a roasting pan with rock salt and wedge the oysters onto the salt to keep them upright.
6. Place under a hot grill for 2–3 minutes until the tops are lightly browned and then eat immediately.

Glossary

Annual: A plant that germinates from seed, grows, and flowers within a single year.

Anther: The pollen-bearing male part of a flower. A small stem, called a filament, supports the anther. Collectively, anthers are known as stamen.

Axil: The junction between a leaf and stem, from where side shoots or flowers may develop.

Basal leaves: These grow around the bases of plants and sometimes differ in size and shape from the ones that appear higher up and attached to the stem.

Berry: A fleshy or succulent fruit with small seeds, such as currants, grapes, gooseberries, and tomatoes.

Biennial: A plant that takes two seasons to complete its life cycle and to produce seeds. In the first year, seeds are sown, they germinate, grow, and produce plants. In the second year, the same plant produces flowers, seeds, and then dies.

Blanching: The exclusion of light from the stems of some vegetables to whiten them and improve their flavor.

Bletted: A process used with certain fleshy fruits when they are allowed to ripen to a point at which they start to decay and ferment. The Medlar (*Mespilus germanica*) is an example where the fruits are allowed to become bletted before being eaten.

Bud: A tightly-packed and closed immature shoot or flower.

Bulb: A swollen, underground, food-storage organ with a bud-like structure. It is formed of fleshy scales attached to a flattened stem called a basal plate.

Bulbils: Small, immature bulbs found around the bases of some bulbs. They can be detached, sown, and encouraged to form roots. Some leaves produce bulbils.

Bracket fungi: Type of fungi with a shelf-like fruiting body that grows on tree trunks and other surfaces, rather than growing in soil at ground-level.

Calyx: The outer ring of a flower, usually green, which protects the flower when it is in bud.

Catkin: A dense, unisexual flowering arrangement. Those on hazels are pendulous, but with willows they are erect.

Cladode: A flattened, leaf-like stem.

Clove: A segment of a bulb; frequently used to refer to a small part of a garlic bulb. May also refer to a dried flower bud of the tropical tree *Eugenia caryophyllus*, which is used whole or ground into a spice.

Conifer: Plants with a tree- or shrub-like nature that bear cones, such as with pines, firs, and spruces. Some conifers are evergreen while others, such as larches, are deciduous.

Corm: An underground storage organ formed of a stem base greatly swollen laterally.

Cultivar: A plant raised in cultivation, rather than appearing naturally and without any interference from man. Properly, the vast majority of plants known as varieties should be called cultivars, but the term "variety" is better known and often seen in books, as well as used in general conversation.

Deciduous: A plant that sheds its leaves at the beginning of its dormant season and produces a fresh set during the following year, at the beginning of its growing period. This usually applies to trees, shrubs, and some conifers.

Dormant: Resting period in a plant's life, normally in late autumn and winter in temperate regions, when a plant makes no noticeable growth.

Escapee: A plant grown in cultivation that, having escaped into the wild, establishes itself in the countryside.

Evergreen: A plant that continuously sheds and grows fresh leaves throughout the year; therefore, it always appears to be green. Some shrubs, trees, and conifers are evergreen.

Fines herbes: French term for finely chopped herbs. They are used fresh or dried, as seasonings, and to flavor sauces.

Flora: A book containing information about native plants in a particular region or country. Also used to denote plants in general.

Floret: Usually very small flowers and part of a larger inflorescence.

Flower: Specialized part of a seed-bearing plant and concerned with reproduction.

Genus: A group of plants with similar botanical characteristics. Some genera contain many species, others just one (they are known as monotypic).

Germination: The process that occurs within a seed when given adequate moisture, air, and warmth. The coat of the seed ruptures and a seed leaf (or leaves) grows up toward the light. A root develops at the same time.

Green manuring: The growing of a crop, such as White mustard, that can be subsequently dug into the soil to improve its physical and nutritional qualities.

Herbaceous: A plant that dies down to soil level after the completion of each season's growth, usually in autumn or early winter. During spring of the following year, the plant develops fresh growth.

Herbal: A book containing information about medicinal and culinary herbs, their uses, and properties.

Inflorescence: The part of a plant which bears the flowers.

Lateral: A side-shoot growing from a main stem of a tree or shrub.

Linear leaves: Narrow and often long.

Lobed leaves: Having round projections around their edges or at the top.

Mast: The fruit of trees such as beech, oak, and sweet chestnut.

Naturalized: A plant that has been introduced into another country or area and has established itself as part of the population.

Perennial: Usually used to describe herbaceous plants, but it also applies to any plant that lives for several years, including shrubs, trees, and climbers.

Rhizome: Horizontal, creeping, underground, or partly underground stem that acts as a storage organ. Some can be slender; others are fleshy and thick.

Runner: A shoot that grows along the ground at intervals rooting into the soil.

Saprophytic: A plant that lives on decaying organic material.

Shrub: A woody perennial with stems growing from soil level and without a trunk. Some plants grow as either shrubs or trees.

Species: A group of plants that breed together and have the same characteristics.

Stamen: The male part of a flower, formed of the anthers and filaments.

Stigma: The female part of a flower on which pollen alights.

Stipe: The stem that bears the fruiting, spore-bearing part of a mushroom. It can also apply to the leafstalks on ferns.

Succulent: Usually applied to thick and fleshy leaves and stems. It can also refer to a group of plants with succulent features.

Style: Female part of a flower—the stem that joins the stigma to the ovary.

Taproot: A long, strong, primary root on some plants, often penetrating deep into the soil.

Tree: A woody plant with a single main stem (trunk).

Tuber: A thickened, fleshy root or stem, wholly or partly under the soil's surface.

Variety: Naturally occurring variation within a species. At one time, all variations within a species were known as varieties. Now, correctly, varieties raised in cultivation are called cultivars.

Photo Credits

All illustrations © David Squire (unless otherwise stated)

All images from Shutterstock.com:

Front cover: David Bokuchava (main); Elena Dijour (top right); KPixMining (middle right); emmanuellegrimaud (bottom right); wabeno (tape). **Back cover:** Jolanda Aalbers (top left); Tatjana Baibakova (middle left); petrovichlili (bottom left). **Used throughout:** Artfury (sidebar backgrounds); kuroksta (sidebar icons); Anucha Tiemsom (paper background). **Page 2:** Madeleine Steinbach. **Page 3:** wabeno (tape). **Pages 4–5:** Kateryna Sednieva. **Page 7:** Kate Higgs. **Page 8:** bsd studio (illustration). **Page 10:** Kristi Blokhin. **Pages 12–13:** Madeleine Steinbach. **Page 14:** K Hanley CHDPhoto. **Page 15:** avoferten. **Page 16:** SeDmi. **Page 17:** Bankiras. **Page 18:** demamiel62. **Page 19:** Marian Weyo. **Page 20:** Manfred Ruckszio. **Page 21:** Burhan Oral GUDU (top), IvanaStevanoski (bottom). **Page 22:** Orest Iyzhechka. **Page 23:** Starover Sibiriak. **Page 24:** Manfred Ruckszio. **Page 25:** Furiarossa. **Page 26:** Orest Iyzhechka. **Page 27:** AxOst. **Page 28:** barmalini. **Page 29:** dabjola. **Page 30:** Irina Borsuchenko. **Page 31:** Beliphotos. **Page 32:** lunamarina. **Pages 33:** Scisetti Alfio. **Page 34:** t50. **Page 35:** Ilona5555. **Pages 36:** Martin Fowler. **Page 37:** Scisetti Alfio. **Page 38:** Martin Fowler. **Page 39:** Nick Pecker. **Page 40:** Martin Fowler. **Page 41:** emmanuellegrimaud. **Pages 42–43:** Bowonpat Sakaew. **Pages 44–45:** Madeleine Steinbach. **Page 46:** Orest Iyzhechka. **Page 47:** nnattalli. **Page 48:** Iker Zabeleta. **Page 49:** Nataly Zavyalova. **Page 50:** ingridagrants. **Page 51:** Elza Brook. **Page 52:** weha. **Page 53:** belizar. **Page 54:** marykal. **Page 55:** Constantine Pankin. **Page 56:** PaniYani. **Page 57:** shihina. **Page 58:** spline_x. **Page 59:** voranat (top); wtondossantos (bottom). **Pages 60:** Danny Hummel. **Page 61:** Manfred Ruckszio (top); Edita Medeina (second from top); Paul Maguire (second from bottom); Danny Hummel (bottom). **Page 62:** janaph. **Page 63:** Hortimages. **Page 64:** Walter Erhardt. **Page 65:** guentermanaus. **Page 66:** weha. **Page 67:** NARONG JHANWATTANA. **Page 68:** SeDmi. **Page 69:** Antoniya Kadiyska (top); vvoe (bottom). **Pages 70–71:** Crepesoles. **Page 72:** McGraw. **Page 73:** Karjalainen. **Pages 74–75:** Alexander Prokopenko. **Page 76:** KPixMining. **Page 77:** BBA Photography. **Page 78:** Orest Iyzhechka. **Page 79:** Peter_Fleming. **Page 80:** Yakov Oskanov; Orest Iyzhechka (inset). **Page 81:** Nata Naumovec. **Page 82:** Dajra. **Page 83:** Peter Turner Photography; lorenza62 (inset). **Page 84:** Carey Jaman. **Page 85:** Nata Naumovec. **Page 86:** Manfred Ruckszio. **Page 87:** Kristine Rad. **Page 88:** aga7ta. **Page 89:** Jane Vershinin. **Page 90:** MVolodymyr. **Page 91:** zoryanchik. **Page 92:** nnattalli. **Page 93:** Maya Kruchankova. **Page 94:** Marinodenisenko. **Page 95:** Galumphing Galah. **Page 96:** Simun Ascic. **Page 97:** Peter Turner Photography; marcovarro (inset). **Page 98:** Ivaylo Ivanov. **Page 99:** Peter Turner Photography; fasenda (inset). **Page 100:** New Africa. **Page 101:** petrovichlili. **Page 102:** nitr. **Page 103:** Liliya Kandrashevich. **Page 104:** Julitt. **Page 105:** Jacek Chabraszewski. **Page 106:** Sergey V Kalyakin; Brzostowska (inset). **Page 107:** Gucio_55; Silvia Dubois (inset). **Pages 108–109:** Oksana_Schmidt. **Page 110:** Kennerth Kullman; M. Schuppich (inset). **Page 111:** imageBROKER.com; Orest Iyzhechka (inset). **Page 112:** OlegD. **Page 113:** sunsinger. **Page 114:** Kuttelvaserova Stuchelova. **Page 115:** George Dolgikh. **Pages 116–117:** Alrandir. **Page 118:** PJ Photography; shalom3 (inset). **Page 119:** Anna Gratys; flaviano fabrizi (inset). **Page 120:** Peter Turner Photography; M. Schuppich (inset). **Page 121:** Eton White (top); Heike Rau (bottom). **Page 122:** Peter Turner Photography; Dan74 (inset). **Page 123:** Petair; Matauw (inset). **Pages 124–125:** TSViPhoto. **Page 126:** Svitlyk. **Page 127:** Gumirov. **Page 128:** colftcl. **Page 129:** Jonas Vegele (top); Looka (bottom). **Page 130:** godi photo. **Page 131:** Henri Koskinen (top); bogdan ionescu (middle); Graeme Pearce (bottom). **Page 132:** Lulub (top); ressormat (bottom). **Page 133:** LFRabanedo. **Page 134:** Martin Hibberd. **Page 135:** Ari N (top); Bukhta Yuri (middle); krolya25 (bottom). **Page 136:** Ingrid Pakats. **Page 137:** LFRabanedo. **Page 138:** Tomasz Czadowski. **Page 139:** FotoLot. **Page 140:** Jolanda Aalbers. **Page 141:** Stephan Morris. **Page 142:** Marinodenisenko. **Page 143:** grafvision. **Pages 144–145:** liz seymour. **Pages 146:** Fotimageon. **Page 147:** Nikki Gensert. **Page 148:** Only Fabrizio. **Page 149:** Harmony Waldron. **Page 150:** arousa. **Pages 151:** Nickola_Che. **Page 152:** Fernando Sanchez Cortes. **Page 153:** Artem Nedoluzhko. **Page 154:** NunZero. **Page 155:** f.maliki. **Pages 156–157:** Tatjana Baibakova. **Page 158:** Ingrid Maasik. **Page 159:** Ezume Images. **Page 160:** Jane Rix. **Page 161:** David Pecheux. **Page 162:** Kersti Lindstrom. **Page 163:** Nickola_Che. **Page 164:** Fotimageon. **Page 165:** Picture Partners. **Page 166:** DronG. **Page 169:** Marinodenisenko. **Page 170:** lunamarina.

Index

About the Author

David Squire studied botany and horticulture at the Hertfordshire College of Horticulture and the Royal Horticulture Society's Garden at Wisley, England, where he gained the Wisley Diploma in Horticulture. Also, he was awarded an N.K. Gould Memorial Prize for his collection of herbarium specimens of native plants, which has since been lodged with the Booth Museum of Natural History in Brighton, Sussex, England.

David has been an editorial staff member for several gardening magazines, book publishing companies, and part-work publishers and has written more than 85 gardening and natural history books, which have been translated into several languages and sold in 20 countries throughout the world.